Globalization, Nationalism and the Text of *Kichaka-Vadha*

Globalization, Nationalism and the Text of *Kichaka-Vadha*

The First English Translation of the Marathi Anticolonial Classic, with a Historical Analysis of Theatre in British India

Translated with an Introduction by
Rakesh H. Solomon

ANTHEM PRESS
LONDON · NEW YORK · DELHI

Anthem Press India
An imprint of Wimbledon Publishing Company India Private Limited (WPCIPL)
WPCIPL is a subsidiary of Wimbledon Publishing Company Limited (UK)

This edition first published in India 2015
by ANTHEM PRESS INDIA
www.anthempress.co.in

First published in UK and USA 2014
by ANTHEM PRESS
www.anthempress.com

Cover image: Untitled oleograph, c. 1895, by Raja Ravi Varma (1848–1906)

ISBN-13: 978 93 80601 70 0 (Hbk)
ISBN-10: 93 80601 70 0 (Hbk)

FOR SALE IN SOUTH ASIA ONLY

Digitally Printed at Replika Press Pvt. Ltd

To June

CONTENTS

PREFACE

I wish to thank a number of libraries and state and national government archives that extended many courtesies to me while I consulted materials at their collections for this as well as other projects on theatre in colonial India. I am grateful, above all, to the Maharashtra State Archives, Bombay, for access to Judicial Department Records of the Bombay Presidency. I am very grateful as well to the Mumbai Marathi Grantha Sangrahalaya, and particularly to reference librarian Krushnakant Shinde, for access to Marathi playscripts and production photographs. For giving me of their time and advice, I thank the respective heads of the following institutions: Asiatic Society, Bombay; Asiatic Society, Calcutta; National Library, Calcutta; and National Archives, New Delhi. I also thank the Oriental and India Office Collections, British Library, London, for access to their materials. Finally, I thank the librarians and staff of Interlibrary Loan at Wells Library, Indiana University Bloomington, for their assistance with obtaining print and microfilm material, including a copy of the original 1907 text of *Kichaka-Vadha* from which this translation was made.

I owe a special debt to the National Endowment for the Humanities and the American Institute for Indian Studies for two senior fellowships that provided very generous support for year-long research stays in India. I also wish to register my appreciation to Indiana University Bloomington for several substantial research awards. From among these, I am especially grateful for two New Frontiers in the Arts and Humanities Grants from the Indiana University Lilly Endowment as well as awards from the College Arts and Humanities Institute, the Office of the Vice President for Research, and the President's Council on International Programs.

I also wish to thank the National Science Council of Taiwan and Frank J. Hildy for their invitation to present my Indian theatre research at the weeklong Symposium on Theatre Historiography at Taiwan National University in Taipei. For generous fellowships that encouraged my Indian theatre work at the earliest stage of my career, I wish to record my continued appreciation to the East-West Center at the University of Hawai'i at Mānoa and to the University of California at Davis.

Beyond institutions and agencies, I am obliged to the following friends for their help. I am especially grateful to Marathi theatre aficionado Pramod Mhaiskar for his generous and gracious assistance, despite his own professional obligations. For their exertions in obtaining photographs and scripts, I thank Shweta and Prashant Chavan in Mumbai and Nitin Madhukar Prabhune in Solapur.

My Indian theatre work has been sustained by both the extraordinary professional generosity and the pioneering scholarship of Phillip Zarrilli, John Emigh, Farley Richmond and Kathy Foley. For that, and for their support in myriad ways and over many years, I wish to record my profound gratitude. For invitations to contribute essays on Indian theatre historiography, I thank Thomas Postlewait and Steve Wilmer (*Writing and Rewriting National Theatre Histories*), Christopher Balme (*Theatre Research International*), Ching-Hsi Perng (*In Search of the Historical Scene: Perspectives on Theatre Historiography*), and Nandi Bhatia (*Modern Indian Theatre: Colonial Encounters and Contested Formations*). I am also grateful to several professional organizations for allowing me to refine my work through public presentation and discussion. My greatest debt is to ASTR (American Society for Theatre Research) for invitations to present at its annual plenary sessions in New York City, Minneapolis, New Orleans, Durham and Philadelphia. While I cannot list here all the societies that afforded me such occasions, I must mention the following that offered me multiple opportunities: ATHE (Association for Theatre in Higher Education), AAP (Association for Asian Performance), Annual Conference on South Asia, MLA (Modern Language Association), and IFTR (International Federation for Theatre Research).

Since I work as much in American theatre as I do in Indian theatre, I would be remiss if I did not acknowledge at least some of my most important debts to my Americanist colleagues. For their generosity and support at some crucial junctures, I am especially grateful to Lincoln Konkle, David Crespy, and Matthew Roudané. I also wish to thank them as well as Stephen Bottoms, John Clum, Jeanmarie Higgins, Cecily Hill, Billy Middleton, Gerald Weales and William Demastes for their generous assessments of my book *Albee in Performance*. For invitations to write essays for their respective volumes, I thank Bruce Mann (*Casebook on Edward Albee*) and Stephen Bottoms (*Cambridge Companion to Edward Albee*).

At Indiana University Bloomington, I thank the India Studies Program for the interdisciplinary exchange it has fostered by regularly bringing together South Asia experts from a range of fields in the US and abroad. For camaraderie beyond my Department of Theatre and Drama, I am grateful to many colleagues in the three academic units I am affiliated with: India Studies Program, Department of Comparative Literature and Cultural Studies Program. It is a pleasure to recall the friendship of several Indiana University colleagues, both past and present, especially Susan and John Samuel, Pravina Shukla, Henry Glassie, Prema and Bill Popkin, Marsha Minton, Steve Raymer, Barbara Skinner, Michael Dodson, Murray McGibbon, Claire and Gerald Larson, and Mala and Kumble Subbaswamy.

During research and other travel over the last several years, I have incurred the debt of many friends and relatives. So it is a very special pleasure to thank them and to replay some fond memories, most particularly of the superb food and easy laughter of June's mother, Agnes, in her Calcutta home. For their hospitality and enduring friendship, I thank Vinita and Amar Singh in Menlo Park, Shamim and Kaiz Poonawala in Austin, Cellie and Ronnie and Molly and Ronald in Mangalore, Mr. and Mrs. Benjamin and Amisha and Gopal Shah in Dohad, Fatima Ghosh and family in Calcutta, and Sumita and Vinod Mehta in New Delhi.

I am grateful to my family for their understanding while I pursued this work. I owe special thanks to my sister Rita, her husband Vijay Somgal and my nephew Raunak for sharing a number of their Marathi contacts. For their moral support, I thank my sister Rekha and my brother Felix and his wife Susan and my nieces Asha and Aneesha in San Francisco. For debts whose import becomes clearer still with the passage of time, I must thank my parents Gulab and Horace. For some inherited affinity to Marathi, I should thank my grandparents Prem and Bala Ram Solomon and particularly my great-grandfather whom family tradition recalls as a Sanskrit scholar from the Maratha Holkar court.

Finally, and most crucially, my deepest debt of all is to my wife June who supported this enterprise with characteristic enthusiasm. For this – and for her support for my several endeavors over so many years – I remain truly grateful.

Part I

Globalization, Nationalism and Theatre in British India

THE HISTORICAL TERRAIN OF *KICHAKA-VADHA*

Sawai Mahavraowancha Mrityu (The Death of Sawai Madhavrao, 1893)

K. P. Khadilkar: Life in Theatre and History

Krishnaji Prabhakar Khadilkar was born on 25 November 1872 in the small Indian principality of Sangli that boasted a rich cultural history and a claim as the birthplace of modern Marathi drama.[1] Following high school Khadilkar studied at the Deccan College in Poona, one of the oldest institutions of modern Western education in India founded in 1821 by the liberal Orientalist and education reformer Mountstuart Elphinstone. At this distinguished college in the

1 In all quoted material in the following pages, I have retained each source's original spelling – without any editorial comment. These spellings include multiple variants for Indian names and terms. I have followed this policy in order to convey a flavor of each document's historical period as well as to allow my text to flow without the excessive editorial interruptions that would otherwise have been necessary. Moreover, in my own text, for the sake of consistency – and given the period primarily covered here – I have used colonial-era names for Indian cities, even for those that have been renamed in recent years.

huge colonial administrative unit known as the Bombay Presidency, Khadilkar combined familiarity with ancient Sanskrit literature and culture with proficiency in English, European literary traditions and modern political ideas. Soon after his graduation in 1892 he wrote his first play, *Sawai Mahavraowancha Mrityu* (The Death of Sawai Madhavrao, 1893) that dramatized events from Maratha history but drew imaginatively on several Shakespearean models. Eventually over a career of forty-two years Khadilkar authored a total of fifteen dramatic works – six plays and nine *sangeet nataks* or musical dramas – many of which, but especially *Kichaka-Vadha* (The Slaying of Kichaka, 1907), *Manapman* (Honor and Dishonor,1911) and *Swayamvara* (1916) fused great theatrical entertainment with covert calls for nationalist resistance and enjoyed extraordinary popular success as well as high critical acclaim. Together with his main actor-singer Bal Gandharva, Khadilkar became the principal force in shaping a period now regarded by common consent as the golden age of Marathi theatre.

Khadilkar also studied law and pursued a parallel career as a journalist, political activist and associate of Bal Gangadhar Tilak, the dynamic leader of the radical wing of the Indian National Congress – the chief political organization fighting British rule. Tilak was a scholar, philosopher, mathematician, and, above all, a towering nationalist leader who laid the groundwork for India's independence and whose strategies inspired Mahatma Gandhi. Popularly called Lokamanya, or Revered by the People, Tilak was acknowledged as "the Father of the Indian Revolution" by Jawaharlal Nehru, independent India's first prime minister. Tilak picked Khadilkar to serve as an editor at two weekly newspapers he owned, the Marathi-language *Kesari* (The Lion) and the English-language *Mahratta*. In 1892 *Kesari* enjoyed the largest circulation among vernacular newspapers in India.[2] Both these publications were geared to rally mass political opposition against colonial rule, and for their pronouncements in these newspapers Tilak and Khadilkar were at different times imprisoned on charges of sedition and conspiracy against the state.

Khadilkar went on to serve as the chief editor of *Mahratta* from 1908 to 1910. After 1910, however, he withdrew from both newspapers. In 1917 he returned to edit the *Kesari* for three more years, and upon Tilak's death in 1920 he took over the editorship of the *Lokamanya* until 1923. That year he founded and edited a new daily called *Navakal* – a newspaper that is still published in Bombay and that still gets embroiled in skirmishes with political personalities and government authorities from time to time, as happened recently when its editorial against a state politician led to an attack on its offices.[3]

Given his close and longstanding association with Tilak, the most frequent epithet for Khadilkar today in both popular as well as scholarly writing is "Tilak's lieutenant." It was a label that colonial authorities themselves had pinned on him

2 Brown, 77.

3 "Rane 'supporters' attack Marathi daily office over editorial," *Times of India*, 22 January 2009. Six years earlier the editor of *Navakal* was imprisoned for seven days on charges of contempt of court for publishing editorials critical of a judge: see "*Navakal* editor jailed," *Times of India*, 16 July 2003.

Sawai Mahavraowancha Mrityu (The Death of Sawai Madhavrao, 1893)

as early as 1917: a biographical sketch prepared for the Government of Bombay lists him prominently – right behind the leader's main relatives – as one of Tilak's principal "lieutenants."[4] Given this connection, it is no surprise that most Khadilkar plays – whether set in historical, contemporary, or mythical locales – grapple directly or indirectly with his era's political or social issues. In *A History of Marathi Literature* Kusumawati Deshpande and M.V. Rajadhyaksha suggest that for Khadilkar "writing for the stage was a part of his larger mission: to teach the people, and the teaching was moral as well as political [...] He was, in a sense, a journalist first, and everything else afterwards."[5] Although this might overstate the case somewhat, their assessment of the source of his rhetorical power is quite accurate: "The telling prose of his plays came from the journalist in him – as also, if a little, from the public speaker in him."[6]

It is this rhetorical power to move an audience in the cause of a radical nationalist program, a program deemed terrorism by colonial authorities, that makes his best known play *Kichaka-Vadha* so successful as a piece of political theatre – and that once rendered it so dangerous to the British. Coupled with the rhetorical prowess is his dramaturgy that crafts characters and events that emerge from considered

4 Judicial Department, No. 3074/H/l, Maharashtra State Archives, Bombay.

5 Deshpande and Rajadhyaksha, 113–14.

6 Deshpande and Rajadhyaksha, 114.

Swayamvara (1916)

and volitional action – not from accidents of fate, history or convention. By portraying human beings and situations in this manner, he demonstrates to the audience the possibility and efficacy of political action. "The audience, therefore," as distinguished Marathi fiction writer and critic Gangadhar Gadgil points out, "comes away with the conviction that [...] they themselves could mould and shape their own lives, and their future too, whichever way they wished."[7] Audience reaction, in fact, was specifically cited by the government as a justification for banning *Kichaka-Vadha*, a topic discussed at greater length in the subsequent paragraphs. Quoting from a Secret Police Abstract, dated 13 November 1909, a police commissioner makes his case, "There is no doubt that a Deccan audience takes [the play] as a cleverly-veiled incitement to murder European officials."[8]

As nationalist ideologies and practices evolved in the 1920s, the independence movement turned away from advocating a violent overthrow of the government in favor of Mahatma Gandhi's call for *Satyagraha*, that is, peaceful non-cooperation with the institutions and laws of the British Raj. Khadilkar now harnessed his

7 Gangadhar Gadgil, *Khadilkaranchi Teen Nataken* [Khadilkar's Three Plays] (Pune: Vimal Prakashan, 2nd ed., 1990, 12); quoted in Gokhale, 30.

8 In this and the next paragraph all information and quotations come from Judicial Department Records, No. 503 of 1910; Letter No. C. 4-Confl., 14 January 1910; Maharashtra State Archives.

Swayamvara (1916)

rhetorical and dramaturgic craft to advocate the new agenda in plays like *Menaka* (1926) and *Savitri* (1933) that virtually embody the tenets of *Satyagraha*. He also used his newspaper *Navakal* to rally public opinion behind Gandhi's movement. Despite this commitment to non-violent action, he was imprisoned on charges of sedition in 1927 and again in 1929.

Khadilkar's achievement as a playwright and journalist were marked by many public honors. He was fêted by prestigious theatrical and literary organizations with invitations to preside over gatherings like the Natya Sammelan (Theatre Symposium) in 1907, the Sangeet Parishad (Music Drama Council) in 1921, and Sahitya Sammelan (Literary Symposium) in 1933. He withdrew from politics in 1936 and devoted himself to meditation and philosophical writings that included several commentaries on Hindu religious texts. Khadilkar savored, albeit briefly, the success of his lifelong devotion to the nationalist cause when India secured independence in 1947, a year before his death in Poona at the age of seventy-six.

Historical and Theatrical Topography

Extending the perspective considerably beyond that provided by the crucial but necessarily circumscribed particulars of a personal history and career, I will in the following section situate *Kichaka-Vadha* within the historical contours of the formation of a new genre called the modern Indian theatre that first emerged in the eighteenth century. This genre was urban and elite, interwove European and indigenous theatre practices and focused frequently on current social and political issues through a lens of contemporary global developments and ideologies. I will next locate the play within the stream of nationalist resistance that soon began to course within this new genre and that by the late decades of the nineteenth and early twentieth centuries became decisively militant in the theatre of the Marathi-speaking Deccan region of western and central India.[9] I will further underscore *Kichaka-Vadha's* historical foundation by placing it within a matrix of dramatic works that were considered so subversive that their publication or production was prohibited or their playwrights, actors or publishers prosecuted in the courts or punished with various administrative sanctions by the government of the Bombay Presidency. I will conclude with an analysis of how Khadilkar transformed Book IV of the *Mahabharata*, an ancient Hindu epic, into one of the most explosive works of political theatre staged during the British Raj. Such an overview of *Kichaka-Vadha's* historical and theatrical terrain will have the added advantage of offering a glimpse of the salient features of the pre-independence modern Indian theatre, its influential role in the resistance against imperial rule, and, above all, the considerable artistic achievement of the group of playwrights who created the early twentieth-century efflorescence of modern Marathi drama – subjects that, compared to the relatively well known traditional genres of Indian theatre, deserve to be more widely known not only in the West but also in India.

Proto- and Modern Globalizations: Emergence and Expansion of the Modern Indian Theatre

Recently an influential group of Cambridge historians has offered a preliminary but persuasive taxonomy and periodization for the study of globalization in a volume entitled *Globalization in World History*.[10] These scholars of globalization have suggested four principal, if overlapping and interacting, historical manifestations of the phenomenon as archaic, proto-, modern, and postcolonial globalizations. They label the period roughly between 1750 and 1850 as the era of proto-globalization. Those are precisely the years that witnessed the birth and early development of the modern Indian theatre – during the first substantial and extended phase of the historical encounter between India and Europe. The beginning of that phase can be traced to 1757 when soldiers of the world's first multinational corporation, the East India Company, defeated the ruler of Bengal, Nawab Siraj-ud-daula, in the decisive Battle of Plassey that soon became the historic signpost for the establishment and expansion of British territorial power in Eastern India. The Plassey triumph also signaled the success of the East India Company over the French East India Company, which had backed Siraj-ud-daula, as the two companies had extended eighteenth-century Europe's Anglo-French conflicts into India, establishing rival settlements and impacting regional power holders as well

9 Some parts of the following discussion, in an early version, appeared in *Theatre Journal* 46, no. 3: 323–47.

10 A. G. Hopkins.

as local cultures. The Cambridge globalization historians designate the hundred years or so that followed proto-globalization, that is, the period approximately between 1850 and 1950, as the age of modern globalization. In the case of India, this period of modern globalization coincides with the era of direct rule over the country by the British Government, an era that began in 1858 with the liquidation of the East India Company and ended in 1947 with Indian independence. It was during this period that the modern Indian theatre matured and expanded across major urban centers and regions, establishing professional theatre companies, constructing theatre buildings, and creating an array of new plays and productions for a growing and varied audience. The modern Indian theatre was thus born and raised within the crosscurrents of proto-globalization and modern globalization, which, in India, included two centuries of direct, widespread and deep influence of European governmental and civic institutions and social and cultural practices. As a result the modern Indian theatre – whether the Bengali theatre in Calcutta, the Marathi theatre in the Deccan, the Tamil theatre in Madras, or the Hindi-Urdu theatre in north India – was inevitably marked by an intermingling of European and Indian texts, techniques, and practices. Just as inevitably, given the realities of the colonial enterprise and the local resistance to it, this theatre was marked by striking signs of contestation between imperialist and nationalist agendas, which were, in turn, animated to different degrees by the growing globalization of ideologies, especially those of revolutionary nationalism, in the nineteenth century.

The first direct impact of European theatre in India occurred primarily through the theatrical activities of the resident merchants, military officers, soldiers and others employed or associated with the East India Company. These international entrepreneurs and theatrical enthusiasts built the first European-style theatre in Calcutta in 1753 and named it simply the Play House, reflecting in part the singularity of the structure.[11] As a symbolic portent of the volatile encounter between theatrical performance and state power that would occur in the modern Indian theatre, Nawab Siraj-ud-daula used this theatre building as a prominent offensive post during his siege of Calcutta in 1756, a siege that was ended by the historic Battle of Plassey. Some years later the city saw the inauguration of its second European theatre, an event published in the *London Chronicle*, when Colonel Ironsides "proclaimed, 'BENGAL, to victory thus too long a prey,/At length to wit and taste ha' fought her way'" in his Prologue "at the opening of the Theatre at Calcutta, in Bengal, Dec. 21, 1773."[12]

11 There are slight variations in the dates of the founding of the first theatres: see Guha-Thakurta, 40, for alternative but less convincing dates. For more information on the early theatre in Bengal, see Bharucha, Chatterjee, Das Gupta (vol. 1), Gargi, Guha-Thakurta, Mukherjee, Raha, and Yajnik.

12 *London Chronicle*, 10–13 December 1774. I part company with previous theatre historians in designating the Theatre at Calcutta as the second playhouse, as distinct from the similar-sounding Calcutta Theatre cited by them as the city's second playhouse. I base my conclusion on an analysis of data in Highfill et al. and the *London Chronicle*, neither of which was used by the others.

The architecture, machinery and staging practices of these theatres were modeled after those common in Europe at that time. The Calcutta playhouses contained a pit, gallery and boxes; proscenium stages; painted perspective scenery; shutters and wings; drop and front curtains; and chandeliers and footlights. They offered plays then popular on the London and English provincial stages; their audiences as well as casts consisted exclusively of local British residents; all parts at first were played by men; and the whole enterprise was managed by British personnel – down to ushers and doorkeepers. Within a few years, however, select members of the local Bengali elite were invited to some of these productions, initiating a contact that would eventually culminate in the formation of a new hybrid theatre genre that is now known as the modern Indian theatre. By the end of the eighteenth century, with extensive coverage of British theatre productions in local newspapers and periodicals and with an increasing perception of the importance of the English language, influential members of the Bengali elite sought to organize similar theatres and performances of their own.

A Russian-English-French-Bengali-Hindustani Production

These developments led to the first production of the modern Indian theatre on 27 November 1795. On that day Calcutta witnessed a Bengali-language play performed by Bengali actors and musicians in a theatre building expressly constructed for a Bengali audience. Yet this was not a one-culture event: the production, in fact, intertwined multiple elements from Bengali as well as European theatre traditions to create a new hybrid work that captured the essence of that particular globalized historical and cultural moment in colonial India. Translated into Bengali as *Kalpanik Sambadal*, the one-act play was a reimagining of Richard Paul Jodrell's three-act play *The Disguise* published in London in 1787, which was itself derived – via another English adaptation – from French playwright Marivaux's 1730 comedy, *Le Jeu de l'amour et du hazard*.[13] The Bengali reworking of the French-British originals was made by a Russian named Gerasim Steppanovich Lebedev (1749–1817), a violinist, bandmaster, linguist and pioneer Indologist who had arrived in Calcutta eight years earlier. For a planned subsequent offering Lebedev transformed another English play, *Love's the Best Doctor*, also an adaptation of a French comedy, Moliere's *L'Amour Medicin*, which, unfortunately, he had to later abandon. In late 1797 or early 1798 Lebedev left India for London, where he published *A Grammar of the Pure and Mixed East Indian Dialects* in 1801, and eventually returned to St. Petersburg where he worked as a translator in the Ministry of Foreign Affairs and continued his Indological work.

The Bengali *Disguise* was, moreover, a transcultural collaboration between Lebedev, his local tutor Golaknath Das who first suggested and then assisted

13 Jodrell's play was based on William Popple's adaptation, *The Double Deceit: or, A Cure for Jealousy* staged in London at the Theatre Royal in Covent Garden in 1735 and at the Theatre Royal Drury Lane in 1736, and published in London in 1736. For adaptations of Marivaux's play by Popple as well as several other English authors, see Robert Halsband, 20–21.

with the stage performance, and "several learned Pundits who perused the work attentively" and whose reactions Lebedev weighed with great care.[14] Other details also point to a hybrid theatrical production. In his Introduction to *A Grammar of the Pure and Mixed East Indian Dialects* Lebedev writes that "Golucknat-dash, my Linguist [...] engage[d] to supply me with actors of both sexes from among the natives," and "in three months [...] I had both Theatre and Actors ready for my representation."[15] He followed Russian, French, and British examples of theatre architecture to construct a new building with boxes, pit, and gallery – in contrast to local folk theatre practice of performing in any open space, whether outdoor or indoor. As he wrote in his Preface to *The Impartial Observations on the Brahamanian Systems in Eastern India* published in Russian in St. Petersburg in 1805: "Just like my countryman Volkov of Yaroslav, I tried in Calcutta, as if in Moscow, to decorate the floor reserved for staging scenes with painting," but, he emphasized, "according to Bengali taste."[16] Incorporating traditional Hindu patterns, "the stage was decorated with red-and-yellow religious motifs," and advertised in the *Calcutta Gazette* as the "New Theatre in the Doomtullah Decorated in the Bengalee Style."[17] Within this playhouse, which he named the Bengallie Theatre, Lebedev employed European management practices of charging admission ("Boxes and Pit [...] Sicca/Rs. 8; Gallery [...] Sicca/Rs.4") – as opposed to the local theatre convention of free performances – and announcing the production in a local newspaper, the *Calcutta Gazette* of 5 November 1795. The first performance of *Kalpanik Sambadal* was so well received that four months later for its second staging on 21 March 1796 "the number of subscribers [was] limited to two hundred" from the original performance's three hundred, and the admission price raised steeply to "One Gold Mohur a ticket," as announced in the *Calcutta Gazette* of 10 March 1796.

Lebedev and his collaborators also radically altered the work for a Bengali audience. They moved the play's setting from the original's Madrid and Seville to Calcutta and Lucknow, changed the characters' names and personalities to Indian ones, expanded or reduced the role of some characters, and introduced "watchmen, *chokeydars*; savoyards, *canera*; thieves, *ghoonia*; lawyers, *gumosta*; and amongst the rest a corps of petty plunderers."[18] Such transformations of the European original were driven by pragmatic calculations of what they thought would be theatrically effective in the context of local culture and taste. For instance, Lebedev explained that he inserted sundry

14 Lebedev, vii. I use the terms "transcultural" and "intercultural" broadly to mean the flow of ideas between cultures; the interculturalism of the modern Indian theatre I discuss in this introduction lies closest to category four in the seven-part spectrum of intercultural theatre elaborated by Marvin Carlson on the basis of Michael Gissenwehrer's work: "The foreign and familiar create a new blend, which then is assimilated into the tradition, becoming familiar;" Fischer-Lichte, Riley and Gissenwehrer, 50.

15 Lebedev, vii–viii.

16 Quoted in Saha, "Gerasim Steppanovich Lebedev," in *A Grammar of the Pure and Mixed East Indian Dialects*, ed. Saha, xxxv.

17 Gargi, 108; 5 November 1795.

18 Lebedev, vii.

comic characters into the action because he had "observed that the Indians preferred mimicry and drollery to plain grave solid sense, however purely expressed."[19] The production "commenc[ed] with Vocal and Instrumental Music, called THE INDIAN SERENADE," incorporated Hindustani music, used both Indian and European musical instruments, introduced "the words of the much admired Poet *Shree Bharat Chondra Ray* [...] set to Music," and topped it all off with "Some amusing curiosities" between the acts.[20] For the play's second performance Lebedev offered his audience – made up of Bengalis as well as Europeans – an advance printed "account of the plot and scenes of the Dramas."[21] Moreover, he expanded his initial one-act version into a tri-lingual, Indian-European, three-act work – with the first act in Bengali; the second act's scene one in Hindustani, scene two in Bengali, and scene three in English; and the final act entirely in English.[22] Hindustani as India's lingua franca was understood by Bengalis as well as city residents coming from other regions. Thus the enterprising Russian's choice of a Bengali-Hindustani-English production illustrates both the demographic and cultural mix of a colonial Indian city and the producer's desire for attracting the largest audience and maximizing returns on investment.

The Indian features – decorative, musical, and literary – came from the so-called "classical" traditions of the cultural leaders of Bengal, the *Bhadralog* or upper crust Bengalis who largely regarded popular or folk traditions – including the theatrical forms Kabir Ladai, Panchali, Tarja, and Jatra – to be vulgar and "degenerate entertainment fit only for the lower orders."[23] Consequently, the transcultural exchange that characterized the modern Indian theatre in Bengal generally did not include local non-elite theatre traditions. Later, however, especially given the popularity of Jatra in the regions as well as in Calcutta, the folk theatres' impact on the new hybrid theatre was inevitable, even if it was not programmatic, self-conscious, or acknowledged.[24] The absence of a significant role by folk theatre genres in the early development of the modern Indian theatre coincides with the virtual absence of a pre-colonial history in Calcutta and Bombay where this theatre evolved independently: both cities were largely created by the East India Company's business and administrative exigencies. In contrast, many playwrights

19 Lebedev, vii.

20 *Calcutta Gazette*, 5 November 1795.

21 *Calcutta Gazette*, 10 March 1796.

22 Program for the performance on 21 March 1796, quoted in Nair, "Lebedeff's Life in Calcutta," in *A Grammar of the Pure and Mixed East Indian Dialects*, ed. Saha, xiv; program cover page reproduced in Chatterjee, 29. Lebedev's program uses "Moors" to refer to Hindustani, a common usage among Europeans then.

23 Raha, 8.

24 For alternative views on the role of folk traditions in the growth of the modern Bengali theatre, see Raha, 3–11, and Chatterjee. For a discussion of its influence on postcolonial Bengali theatre, see Bharucha, 90–94. The folk theatre's influence grew considerably during the twentieth century and especially after independence when adapting folk theatre conventions became one of the postcolonial Indian theatre's defining features. Also, note that the distinction between high and low culture and its terminology, according to recent subaltern research discourse, are themselves the result of the imposition of imperial culture on the Indian imagination.

of the modern Indian theatre proudly borrowed elements from the Sanskrit drama that had flourished approximately between the second century B.C.E. and the tenth century C.E. In their embrace of Sanskrit dramatic conventions, they were influenced in part by Europe's recent discovery and high valuation of ancient Hindu texts that arose from the globalization of knowledge starting in the late eighteenth century.[25]

Transcultural Exchange: Theatres, Casts and Plays

Although East India Company politics and machinations of company-connected theatrical entrepreneurs ended Lebedev's enterprise after only two performances, British playhouses prospered. In the early decades of the nineteenth century, upper- and middle-class Bengalis – with rising prosperity, spreading English education, and improving relations with the British – began to attend the English theatres. In 1813 Dwarkanath Tagore, grandfather of Nobel laureate Rabindranath Tagore, became the first Bengali to buy a founding membership in a private English theatre, the Chowringhee Theatre. In 1831 another Bengali became the first to establish a private playhouse, the Hindoo Theatre, in his garden-house to stage English-language plays. In 1848 the *Bengal Hurkaru and India Gazette* announced "the long looked for *debut* of a native amateur in the character of Othello," when Baishnav Charan Adhya played opposite the English Desdemona of a Mrs. Anderson at the Sans Souci Theatre, and the event, according to a letter in the *Calcutta Star*, set "the whole world of Calcutta agog."[26] English-language publications like the *Calcutta Star* and *The Bengal Hurkaru and India Gazette* offered the Adhya-Anderson production qualified praise but considerable coverage.

Within a decade the *Education Gazette* of 13 March 1857 celebrated the first *original* Bengali play to be staged in a private theatre, Ramnarayan Tarkaratna's *Kulinkulasarvasva*, a drama advocating social reforms. By the next decade performances of Bengali plays in private theatres became fairly common, cultural leaders instituted competitions for original Bengali plays, and newspapers regularly urged the establishment of a Bengali *public* theatre. Neatly bringing full circle the process of intercultural exchange, Michael Madhusudan Dutt translated a Bengali script, Tarkaratna's *Ratnabali*, for an English audience in 1858.[27]

25 The Sanskrit play *Abhijnanasakuntala* by Kalidasa, to cite one instance, was published in an English translation in Calcutta (1789), London (1790 and 1792) and Edinburgh (1796), followed by translations in German (1791), Danish (1792), French (1803) and Italian (1815). On the role of European Indology in shaping the historiography of the modern Indian theatre, see Solomon, 3–30.

26 *The Bengal Hurkaru and India Gazette*, 12 August 1848; *Calcutta Star*, 20 August 1848. That the letter also referred to the actor as "a real unpainted nigger Othello" points to another, racial dimension in the complex mix of cultures in colonial India. In addition, for opposing views on the subject of political and cultural hegemony through Shakespearean productions during the British Raj, see Frost, 90–100, and Singh, 445–58.

27 Forty-one new Bengali plays were written in a three-year period from 1869 to 1871, and twenty-six plays were published in 1872 alone, the year of the opening of the first public theatre, the National (Raha, 25).

First Play of Political Protest

Just a year later in 1859 Dinabandhu Mitra wrote *Nil Durpan* (The Indigo Mirror), the first Bengali play of political protest against British atrocities in India. Published anonymously in 1860 and staged in 1861 in Dacca, its author, a senior officer in the colonial administration, however, disavowed any wider anti-British political intent beyond the censure of British indigo planters (his anonymous publication notwithstanding).[28] Although it is now usually labeled a play of "social protest," *Nil Durpan* should more properly be designated as a play of political resistance because it explicitly and graphically located its characters' plight in the systematic, widespread and ruthless exploitation on British indigo plantations that led to the peasants' Indigo Revolt or Blue Mutiny in 1860.[29] Even the British Parliament and the colonial government of Bengal treated the play's publication as a grave political matter, as evident from various communications now available in colonial archives.[30] Thus the circumstances of its birth made the modern Indian theatre not only intercultural but, as exemplified by *Nil Durpan*, quickly political as well.

Modern Marathi Theatre

The development of the modern Indian theatre in the Marathi-speaking regions of the Bombay Presidency occurred along similar lines. Theatre historians usually cite *Sita Swayamvara* (1838) as marking the birth of this modern Marathi theatre and dub its author, Vishnudas Bhave, the father of this genre. In *A History of Marathi Literature*, for instance, Deshpande and Rajadhyaksha assert, "By common consent the history of the Marathi stage begins with the performance of Vishnudas Bhave's *Seetaswayamwar*."[31] The first production of the Marathi theatre also embodied the interplay of politics and culture. The commission for *Sita Swayamvara* was issued by the ruler of the small princely state of Sangli, Raja Appasaheb Patawardhan, a well-known patron of the arts, with the explicit goal of creating a new performance that would "clean up" and "refine" what he condemned as the crude depiction of Hindu deities in the Bhagavata Mela, a traditional folk dance theatre genre from the nearby Kannada-language area of North Canara. The Raja's project seems aimed at least in part to resist widespread British claims of cultural superiority over the Maratha royal houses. As a member of the generally well-heeled and well-traveled Indian aristocracy, he had most likely witnessed or at least known of English

28 *Bengal Hurkaru*, 12 June 1861; Chatterjee, 171, 222. While the vast majority of indigo planters were British, a few were rich Bengali landowners, Chatterjee, 224.

29 Some scholars like Guha and Chatterjee question such a designation because the play calls for reforms within the framework of colonial rule, but the author's stance may conceivably have been a matter of pragmatic expedience for a civil servant; and, more crucially, a revolutionary ideology is not the sole criterion that makes a play political.

30 For example, see Gopal, 22–3.

31 Deshpande and Rajadhyaksha, 110. For further discussion of Bhave's claim to that title, see Desai, 16–17, Rangacharya, 95–97, and Gokhale, 1–11.

Kanchangadchi Mohana (Mohana of Kanchangad, 1898)

theatre performances. By staging in his court a unique, new-style performance of his own cultural heritage, he asserted his refined taste and co-equal status with the British as well as demonstrated to his subjects and neighboring rulers his dedication to Hindu deities and to the cultivation of local cultural forms. With *Sita Swayamvara* it is also clear that in the founding of the modern Marathi theatre, in contrast to that of the modern Bengali theatre, a folk genre – albeit from a neighboring region – played an important part. However, despite this initial connection to a folk genre, the Marathi cultural elites – writers, actors, and producers who developed the modern theatre in the Bombay Presidency – did not directly mine their own local folk forms. As a result the robust Marathi folk theatres like *Gondhal*, *Kirtana*, *Lalita*, *Powada* and *Tamasha* did not significantly impact the modern Marathi theatre until after independence.

As distinct from *Sita Swayamvara* – with its preponderance of verse, songs and spectacle – the first Marathi "prose play," or a play written entirely in prose, was Vinayak Janardan Kirtane's 1860 work, *Thorle Madhavrao Peshwe* (The Elder Mahavarao Peshwa).[32] The popular genre of "prose plays" that this work initiated became known, not without some pejorative connotation, as "bookish plays." Such plays were especially prized by the emerging Westernized Marathi intelligentsia. Like *Nil Durpan* in the Bengal Presidency, *Thorle Madhavrao Peshwe* was a play of political protest against British domination and injustice in the Bombay Presidency.

32 Theatre histories in Marathi and English date the play's composition variously to 1860 or 1861.

(Parallel historical and cultural developments in the Madras Presidency likewise made the modern Tamil drama political early on: Kashi Viswanatha Mudaliyar's 1858 play *Taciltar Natakam*, for example, satirized malpractices in the British colonial administration.) In *Thorle Madhavrao Peshwe* Kirtane borrowed from European dramatic models, especially Shakespeare, and cloaked his nationalist politics within the form of a historical tragedy. Ostensibly, he was merely dramatizing recent Indian history, namely, the reign of the Peshwas, the last great Maratha rulers; in reality, however, by stressing the contrast between past and present conditions he was advocating the end of foreign rule. Moreover, by glorifying the Peshwas whom the British deposed and vilified, Kirtane championed the cause of the contemporary claimant to the Peshwa throne, Nana Saheb, who was also a leader of the 1857 anti-British uprising and the figure the British accused of ordering the slaughter that became notorious as the Bibighar Massacre. The Bibighar killings became a central element in British representations of India where "Indian savagery" justified brutality and continued rule. In contrast, playing out Anglo-French rivalries noted earlier, contemporaneous French-language texts and images represented the Bibighar Massacre as an instance of Indian revolutionary resistance.[33] Many plays of the period, besides Kirtane's historical drama, condemned the harshness of colonial rule now securely in place through much of India. Growing resistance to that rule turned the 1857 uprising of soldiers or sepoys into the First Indian War of Independence, misnamed by many historians as the Sepoy Mutiny, even though as early as 1859 Viceroy Canning himself characterized it as a "national war [...] in its magnitude, duration, scale [...] and [...] moral features."[34]

As a consequence of the 1857 uprising, and coinciding with the start of the age of modern globalization, the British Parliament passed the Government of India Act of 1858 that transferred the East India Company's power and assets to the Crown and ended the multinational corporation's two-hundred-and-fifty-eight-year checkered history. From then on the country was administered directly by a British secretary of state for India and a governor-general that he appointed. With persisting bitterness on both sides from the savagery of the 1857 war, the next four decades from 1858 to 1898 – i.e., leading up to the time of Khadilkar and the other Marathi playwrights prosecuted by the colonial machinery – witnessed further exacerbation in the relations between the Indians and the British, leading to an increasingly vigorous nationalist resistance and a correspondingly fierce colonial repression. Perhaps the most extensive and extreme anti-colonial movement developed in the Deccan region in the west. By the 1870s the Governor of Bombay complained, "Never have I known in India a national and political ambition so continuous, so enduring, so far reaching, so utterly impossible for us to satisfy as that of the Brahmins of western India."[35] By the first decade of the

33 Frith, 368–82.

34 Gopal, 1. Viceroy Canning also acknowledged the accuracy of the exploitation portrayed in *Nil Durpan*, Gopal, 27–28.

35 Quoted in Seal, 234.

next century, especially after the government's mishandling of the famine of 1896 and the plague outbreak of 1897, the London *Times* could rightly declare on 18 January 1909, "It is well-known that in no part of India, not even in Bengal, is hostility to British rule more widespread or bitter than in the Deccan."

Imperialist and Nationalist Uses of Culture

Significantly contributing to this hostility was the growing encroachment of British authority in most regions of the country and in most aspects of Indian life – exercised through the sweeping imposition of imperial culture, a process that globalization historians consider a classic feature of the era of modern globalization. Chief among the tools for the continuation of empire were: uniform administrative and judicial systems based on British prototypes at both the central and provincial levels, English as the language for all official and therefore nationwide communication, English as the medium of instruction in government as well as private institutions of higher education, and a school and college curriculum of English literature and European social and political history – all accompanied by an implicit or explicit discouragement of Indian languages, history and culture.[36] These steps made an immense impact on Indian society in the second half of the nineteenth century.[37] As an unintended side effect, however, these countrywide measures bolstered the growing sense of pan-Indian nationalism already underway. In a counteroffensive to British cultural imperialism, moreover, nationalist and nativist leaders and writers called for Indian cultural solidarity through a reassertion of pride in the great epochs of Indian history and in India's own cultural traditions, systems and values. In short, they sought to use Indian culture and history to refashion a modern national identity and mobilize nationalist resistance.

New research on the composition of the Indian nationalist leadership has discredited previous views about a monolithic Westernized middle-class elite and rehabilitated the role of vernacular literati, regional power brokers, and Gramscian intellectuals and strategists.[38] Nevertheless, a substantial number of the leaders and their followers – including Khadilkar and several of his fellow Marathi playwrights – were members of an influential bourgeoisie shaped at least in part by the government's introduction of Western education. These nationalists became proficient in English and familiar with English literature as well as European history and political philosophy. Drawing on what one historian has called a "warehouse

36 Ironically, because of its usefulness in the imperialist project, English literature became a curricular subject in India much before it did in England: see Gauri Viswanathan's *Masks of Conquest* for an analysis of the hegemonic function of the curricular introduction of English literature and language in British India. Also, for a critique of institutionalized study of literature in postcolonial India, see Ania Loomba.

37 Following its longstanding strategy, the colonial government, however, did not legislate in the explosive realms of religious and family life.

38 For a succinct overview of scholarship on the subject, see Michelguglielmo Torri, 18–55.

of Western ideas" accessible through European publications and foreign travel, elite leaders sought to mold a modern Indian society that synthesized the best from Europe and from India's own history and culture.[39] Moreover, cognizant of international economic, social and political trends – something made possible by modern globalization – they were equally keen to adapt to nationalist ends European emphasis on science and material progress as well as European political ideologies, as evident in the popularity in both vernacular and English translations of the writings of Voltaire, Rousseau, Garibaldi, Mazzini, and Cavour among educated middle-class Indians.[40] This familiarity with global developments among nationalists is summarized by Sailendra Nath Sen in his *History of Freedom Movement in India (1857–1947)*: "Contemporary international events had made a strong impact on the young patriots. The defeat of the Nationalist Upsurge of the Italians at Adowa in 1894 at the hands of the Abyssinians, the victory of Japan over Russia [in] 1904–1905, the rise of the Sinn Fein movement in Ireland as well as the Young Turk revolt, encouraged patriotic Indians to look forward with confidence. The young conspirators derived inspiration from the *Bhagavad Gita* as well as from the lives of Mazzini, Garibaldi and Russian methods of revolutionary activities."[41]

Operating within this swirl of modern global political developments, Khadilkar and some of his fellow prosecuted Marathi dramatists pursued parallel careers as political journalists at nationalist newspapers. As noted earlier, Khadilkar, the leading playwright of the period, served as an editor at several major news publications like *Kesari*, the foremost Marathi weekly of the time, the *Mahratta*, *Lokamanya*, and his own *Navakal*. Another censored playwright, Anant Vaman Barve, also had an ongoing journalistic career: he worked as an editor at the Marathi daily *Lokseva* (Service of the People) as well as published a monthly magazine devoted to theatre called *Natyakala* (Theatre Arts). In addition, Barve founded the Bharata Natya Samaj (Indian Theatre Society), a leading organization for professional theatre, under whose auspices was held the first Marathi professional theatre conference in Bombay in 1905. Mirroring the period's mix of theatre and politics, the conference was presided over by Dada Saheb Khaparde, an eminent lawyer and, like Khadilkar, a close associate of Tilak.[42]

Several of the prosecuted Marathi dramatists were active participants in the nationalists' project of establishing and running schools and colleges designed to counter the exclusively Western curriculum and methods of government-run educational institutions. Playwright Krishnaji Hari Dikshit ran one such "national school" in Belgaum, which British officials had put on a government blacklist. Like many educated nationalists, three other dramatists found employment only in

39 Wolpert, *Tilak and Gokhale*, 6.

40 I say "adapt" – rather than "adopt" – in order to guard against those who allege that exclusively European concepts of liberty inspired the nationalists and who thus misrepresent India's resistance against imperialism as one more of imperialism's selfless benefactions.

41 Sen, 126–7. Also see Bayly, 355–74, for Mazzini's particular impact on nineteenth-century Indian thought.

42 Desai, 28.

the vast government administration: two were clerks – Anna Martand Joshi in the Government Central Press and Gopal Govind Soman in the Executive Engineer's office in the Public Works Department – and one, G. A. Kane, worked as a typist in the Political Department in the Government Secretariat.

Modern Globalization and Global Melodrama

Aware as well of important global cultural trends – and given the modern Indian theatre's hybrid cultural beginnings – these Westernized, urban, and forward-looking Marathi playwrights turned to nineteenth-century Europe's most successful theatrical form: melodrama. Since "melodrama contains every possible ingredient of popular appeal," writes Michael Booth in *Theatre in the Victorian Age*, "the taste for melodrama was ubiquitous and classless."[43] In an instance of remarkable cultural globalization, melodrama was as widely popular with metropolitan audiences in Bombay and Calcutta as it was in London and Paris or New York and Philadelphia or Sydney and Melbourne. One cultural outcome of Britain's vast empire, as Booth points out, was "the expansion of theatrical horizons to comprehend the whole globe."[44] Discussing the touring patterns of theatrical companies, the British magazine *Theatre* observed in 1882, "The 'circuits' of Bristol, Norwich and York of the last century are now replaced by those of the United States, South Africa, India and Australia."[45] To this list it could have added, among others, Canada, the West Indies, New Zealand and the Far East.

Such worldwide theatrical touring developed in tandem with the rise of trade and transportation networks, especially those of railroads and steamships, that served the enmeshed growth of empire and modern globalization. English touring companies, Booth notes, regularly traveled to "India, landing in Bombay, playing a season there and then taking the long train journey to Calcutta."[46] In fact, these troupes traveled far beyond these two cities: each year when the British moved their Indian capital from Calcutta in the east to Simla in the northwest Himalayan foothills for the summer months, many of these companies – with names like the Dave Carson Company, the Lewis Dramatic Company, the Fairclough Company, and the Loftus Troupe – routinely made the same 3000-mile roundtrip rail journey.[47] Crucially, on both their way to and from Simla they stopped for a few days or a week at a time in smaller cities across central and north India to perform in local theatres and in British civil and military settlements. The Lewis Dramatic Company on its trip from Calcutta to Simla between 28 March and 11 May 1869, for instance, performed in twelve different towns and cities as well as Simla. According to actor William Giles, the company went to "Jamuipore, Dinapore,

43 Booth, 150, 152.

44 Booth, 20.

45 Quoted in Booth, 20.

46 Booth, 21.

47 Gänzl, 39–54.

Prem Dhwaj (Love's Emblem, 1911)

Benares, Allahabad, Cawnpore, Lucknow and Agra, and then on to Meerut and Moosooric in the Himalayas, coming back again to Umballah [...] then Kasonlie, Duckshi and Simla."[48]

Thus many Indian elites in the various regional centers beyond the cities of Bombay, Calcutta and Madras also came under the spell of the global phenomenon of melodramas staged by Europeans in European-style productions. However, a far greater number of Indian theatre practitioners and audiences acquired their taste for melodrama *indirectly* – through the Hindustani-language productions of the Parsi theatre companies that first emerged as amateur troupes in mid-nineteenth-century Bombay. The enterprising Parsi community of Western India that had readily embraced many European social and cultural mores soon established some of the first largely professional theatre companies in India based on contemporary European models of theatrical entrepreneurship.[49] These companies borrowed not only the Europeans' economic practices but, predictably, their writing and staging techniques for melodrama as well.[50]

48 Gänzl, 45–46. On colonial-era spellings in quoted material, see note 1 above.

49 As the dramatist and theatre historian Adya Rangacharya quipped, "Bombay is a commercial centre, the Parsis a commercial community and the professional theatre a commercial venture," Rangacharya, 101.

50 For an excellent summary history of the Parsi theatre, see "Pioneers to Professionals: A Retrospective of the Parsi Theatre," Hansen, 3–25.

Unlike the Marathi and other streams of modern Indian theatre, the Parsi theatre steered clear of politics almost completely because of its focus on commercial success. Concentrating on creating a product with mass appeal, it ingeniously exploited for an Indian audience melodrama's spectacular scenery, special effects, complicated plots, music, dance and extravagant acting. The Parsi theatre's success led to a proliferation of their companies, which traveled across wide swathes of the country spreading the global phenomenon of European-style melodramatic plays and productions. The Parsi companies thus exercised an unprecedented nationwide influence on the style and content of the new modern theatres then emerging in different Indian languages. The Marathi theatre was no exception to this impact: born only a few years earlier, as seen above, it quickly came under the spell of the Parsi theatre. Even Vishnudas Bhave, who created the first Marathi theatre performance in 1838, soon found himself dazzled by Parsi productions he saw in Bombay and began to incorporate into his own productions some of their devices, especially the spectacle made possible by the Parsi companies' scene changing machinery. A theatre historian reviewing the Marathi theatre of the last quarter of the nineteenth century grants that even playwrights "wanting to wean the playgoer away from the Parsi-Urdu theatre, were not averse to using its garish colors."[51] In fact, by the early decades of the twentieth century some Marathi playwrights, in order to maintain a distinct identity, were making serious efforts to eliminate some (though not all) of the Parsi features from their performances. For example, Khadilkar earned plaudits from audiences and newspaper reviewers alike in 1911 when his *Manapman* became the first Marathi sangeet to restrict its songs and melodies to the elite Hindustani "classical" tradition, departing from the common practice of relying on popular musical fare typical of Parsi productions.

Nonetheless, the banned Marathi dramatists at the turn of the century drew significantly on the playwriting and staging methods of the Parsi companies, although many of their appropriations of European theatrical practices came directly from British productions and from their formal study or private reading of printed plays available in India.[52] Crucially as nationalists, they also adopted several elements from ancient Sanskrit plays that had been newly revalued as part of the elites' agenda of bolstering their own cultural heritage. Like the Parsi plays and their European models, these Marathi works – including *Kichaka-Vadha* that exemplifies this drama – followed melodramatic patterns of characterization and plotting: morally unequivocal characters; minimal exposition; fast-moving plots; subplots of love intrigue; act-end climaxes; strict poetic justice; and stock devices of disguise, sudden discovery, abduction and last-minute rescue. Yet, as in the Parsi plays – and as in the early reworkings by Lebedev and others in

51 Deshpande and Rajadhyaksha, 110.

52 Bhave saw a proscenium-style production as early as 1853 when he attended an English-language play in a theatre built by an Indian businessman in Bombay. Within a month of his attendance, he went on to write and stage a new play in that theatre, making it the first Marathi professional and ticketed production in a European-style theatre in Bombay; Gokhale, 7–8.

Bengali – the *specifics* of characters, plots and settings were completely localized: thus these Marathi plays depicted Indian characters in Indian settings, often accompanied by Indian music and dance, and dealt exclusively with Indian concerns and themes. Incorporating Sanskrit theatre traditions, they also included some Hindu rituals: an opening *puja*, an invocation, and a concluding prayer. Additionally, some plays included the Sanskrit theatre's *Sutradhara*, a combination of an on-stage narrator, actor, stage manager and chorus. In matters of staging, again as in the Parsi productions and their European prototypes, they utilized a proscenium stage, illusionistic scenery painted on wings and shutters and on drop and front curtains, some functional furniture, and, often, floor coverings, such as carpets and realistic grass and shrubbery. Some of their playwriting as well as staging features, however, belonged as much to melodrama as to Sanskrit theatre aesthetics and conventions: these common elements included music to underline emotion, tableaus, dance, heightened emotions and stereotypical characters; additionally, most of these shared features maintained distinctly Indian characteristics. Local taste, moreover, required an un-darkened auditorium and an informal atmosphere. In the area of business and organization, these political playwrights and their producers followed the practices of the Parsi and English companies: a pre-announced fixed schedule of performances, admission tickets, and publicity via advertisements and handbills.

Colonial Surveillance and Regulation of Marathi Theatre

A picture of the nationalist resistance advocated in the Marathi melodramas by Khadilkar and his fellow playwrights – as well as a picture of the colonial government's police, administrative and legal response to it – emerges from extensive records, many of them once secret, now available in archives and in post-independence publications. A review of these documents reveals that by the last decade of the nineteenth century, officials of the Bombay Presidency equated most criticism of the British administration with sedition and libel and sought to suppress it through every available avenue. The variety of government documents that focus on these Marathi plays indicates the seriousness of the colonial state's evaluation of the threat from nationalist performances and the corresponding sweep of its surveillance and regulation of theatrical activities in the Bombay Presidency. In fact, the majority of the historical evidence about the Marathi plays and playwrights analyzed here comes from colonial government records. Evidence surfaces in the communications of such offices as those of the Governor of Bombay; the Political Agent of the Deccan States; the Collector of Colaba District; the District Magistrates of Poona, Colaba and Ratnagiri; the Oriental Translators to Government; the Remembrancer of Legal Affairs; even the Public Works Department; but, above all, the different branches of the police departments in various districts of the presidency.

The law that allowed some of this censorship – the Dramatic Performances Control Act XIX of 1876 – was enacted in the Supreme Legislative Council in

Calcutta and was intended "to empower the Government to prohibit Native plays which are scandalous, defamatory, seditious or obscene."[53] If a proscribed play was performed, the law allowed the "police to enter with such assistance as may be requisite, by night or by day, and by force, if necessary, any such house, room or place, and to take into custody all persons whom he finds therein, and to seize all scenery, dresses and other articles found therein."[54] Even while the Supreme Legislative Council was considering the passage of this law, Indians voiced their opposition through public meetings and resolutions in Calcutta, Dacca, Lucknow, Kanpur and Allahabad; through formal petitions by influential Indian landowners and industrialists of the British Indian Association; and through editorials in magazines and newspapers like the Bengali *Amrita Bazar Patrika*, the English-language *Mookerjee's Magazine*, the Gujarati *Bombay Samachar*, and the Marathi *Arunodaya* and *Dnyan Prakash*.[55] The Indian opposition proved no obstacle, and the passage of the new law was cheered by establishment figures and institutions in both India and Britain. Ironically, the *Theatre*, a magazine published from London, was among those cheering: it justified the law by asserting, "The great moral and educational influence exercised by the great theatres of Europe has for some years been almost totally unknown in the East."[56]

By the first decade of the twentieth century, British officials felt that existing statues were proving inadequate and that they needed more robust and comprehensive new laws, especially in view of the growing number of printing presses and the proliferation of anticolonial newspapers, magazines, books, pamphlets, posters, and so on. The officials were particularly attentive to regulating the kind of material that, like the plays under consideration here, resorted to implication and innuendo in place of overt statement in order to stay within the letter of the existing laws. The colonial government consequently crafted a new law, the Indian Press Act, 1910, that empowered local governments "in the whole of British India" to control virtually every form of printed communication. The new statute authorized officials to act against those "printing or publishing any newspaper, book or other document containing any words, signs or visible representations which are likely or may have a tendency, directly or indirectly, whether by inference, suggestion, allusion, metaphor, implication or otherwise" to encourage sedition or disaffection for the government.[57] As is clear from the language of the Indian Press Act, it was specially targeted at writing that operated through inference and indirection.

53 Government Legislative Department, *Unrepealed General Acts*, vol. 2: 74.

54 Government Legislative Department, *Unrepealed General Acts*, vol. 2: 74.

55 *Mookerjee's Magazine*, new series, 5, nos. 36–40 (1876) and *Report on Native Newspapers*, January–June 1876. A number of pro-British Indian establishment figures and publications, however, welcomed the new law, especially on the grounds that it would suppress obscenity and immorality: see, for instance, Kundu, 79–93.

56 "Theatre Legislation in India," *Theatre*, 20 February 1877, 41.

57 India, *Collection of the Acts Passed by the Governor General*, 1, 2–3.

Armed with many such expansive laws, both old and new, the authorities preempted or terminated productions of plays by several of these Marathi dramatists. In 1898 as the playwright-actor Joshi prepared to appear in the titular role of his play *Shri Shiv Chhatrapati Vijaya* (Victory of Shri Shiv Chhatrapati, 1893) at the Alfred Theatre in Bombay, the government's Oriental Translator argued that the play expressed "misfeelings in vehement language regarding the subjection of Hindus to foreign rule, their inherent right to be paramount in their own Fatherland [...] and the desirability of union among the Hindus for the achievement of their political independence."[58] The Commissioner of Police in Bombay ruled that the play was objectionable, summoned the author, found him "amenable to pressure," and made him cancel the production and surrender all 320 printed copies of the play.[59] In addition, the police department began a dossier on Joshi, noted his membership in Hindu religious organizations, added his name to a blacklist, and launched an investigation into his background and current activities.

Similarly, the District Magistrate of Kolaba, Mr. J. K. N. Kabraji, shut down the Mahad city premiere production of Ramchandra Mahadeo Mhaiskar's *Vijaya Torna* (Victory at Torna Fort, 1909), a dramatization of Hari Narayan Apte's historical novel about the rise of Maratha power. Even though the production was being staged by an amateur theatre troupe, the Mahad Manoranjan Natak Company, District Magistrate Kabraji charged the leader of the company, Laxman Vithal Oak, and his fourteen actors under section 102 of the Criminal Procedure Code and made them deposit Rs. 200 each as a surety for good behavior for a year.[60] The size of the required deposit was punitive: the author's monthly salary, for instance, was only Rs. 8 when he began teaching in Sholapur Municipality School No. 6 in 1904, as noted in the intelligence records. Two actors, Keshav Shridhar Chaude and Kashinath Narayan Hardikar, who could not raise the sum were sentenced to one year's rigorous imprisonment. Moreover, within two months the Government of Bombay proceeded to prohibit all future performances of the play, and the Political Agent of the Deccan States seized all five hundred copies of the script when it was published in book form.[61]

When the authorities could not marshal enough evidence to bring charges against a playwright personally under any existing civil or criminal law, they resorted to extrajudicial harassment. Some playwrights, such as Joshi, Mhaiskar, Shankar Sitaram Chitnis and Vasudeo Rangnath Shirvalkar, were called in and issued stern warnings by senior officials; others, such as Soman and Kane, were

58 Judicial Department Records, No. 1086 of 1898, Maharashtra State Archives, Bombay.

59 Judicial Department Records, Volume 178 of 1898, Maharashtra State Archives, Bombay.

60 Judicial Department Confidential Compilation No. 2018, File No. 175 of 1909, Maharashtra State Archives, Bombay.

61 Judicial Department Government Resolution, No. 5931 of 1909, 22 October 1909; Judicial Department Confidential Compilation No. 897, File No. 192 of 1910; Maharashtra State Archives, Bombay.

Prem Dhwaj (Love's Emblem, 1911)

reprimanded by their departmental supervisors and driven to resign from their government jobs. In his letter of resignation to the Executive Engineer of Thana District, dated 1 March 1899, Soman protested, "As I am reprimanded for writing *Bandhavimochan*, a dramatic play, owing to which I am transferred, I beg to resign my services."[62] When the Remembrancer of Legal Affairs decided that a successful criminal prosecution of Kane for his play *Drauni Mani Haran* (Seizing Drauni's Jewel, 1910) was unlikely, the author's supervisors at the Government Secretariat demanded a written undertaking from him promising not to write anything "objectionable" in the future; Kane refused and had to submit his resignation.[63] Even though no criminal proceedings were initiated against the author, the play itself was banned in July 1910.[64]

Kichaka-Vadha: Dramaturgic Smokescreen and Police Dilemma

In the case of Khadilkar's *Kichaka-Vadha* – first staged by the Maharashtra Natak Mandali in 1907 in Poona – government officials remained divided about

62 Judicial Department Records, No. 46 of 1911, Maharashtra State Archives, Bombay.

63 Judicial Department Confidential Compilation No. 1489, File No. 192 of 1910, Maharashtra State Archives, Bombay.

64 Judicial Department Records, No. 3715 of 1910, Maharashtra State Archives, Bombay.

its political import for almost two years, no doubt thrown off by the play's allegorical smokescreen. Although some officials thought it conveyed a seditious message, others viewed it as a drama simply about political infighting within the two camps of the Indian National Congress and thus of no threat to the government. Probably prompted by the work's continuing popularity, the divergent views among officials and the growing police dossier on its author's nationalist activities, the Government of Bombay instructed Deputy Commissioner of Police F. A. M. H. Vincent to attend a performance and submit a report whether or not government action was required.[65] Deputy Commissioner Vincent attended a performance in November 1909 but found nothing meriting continued police reports on the play. However, Commissioner W. T. Morison of the Criminal Division in Bombay still remained uncertain and sought detailed intelligence about the play and its reception through a Brahmin undercover agent with a native command of the Marathi language. The unnamed informant attended two performances in Poona and provided a comprehensive account and analysis, as recorded in the Secret Police Abstract of 13 November 1909. That account when combined with other evidence in secret police files convinced Commissioner Morison that the play's dialogue and plot communicated covert seditious messages, and he soon recommended to the secretary of the Judicial Department in Bombay that *Kichaka-Vadha* be banned.

In his confidential letter to the Judicial Department, Commissioner Morison emphasized that in order to precisely assess the play's political meaning and impact he had picked a Brahmin informant who "cannot be in error as to the way in which the play was received." Rejecting the earlier assessment by Deputy Commissioner Vincent, he emphasized that his informant had attended two performances of *Kichaka-Vadha* and "the impression left on him was different from that which the performance produced on Mr. Vincent." Morison shared his informant's conclusion that "the play, as acted, had distinctly seditious tendency." He also cited further details about audience composition and response supplied by his undercover agent: "The audiences in Poona were composed almost entirely of Brahmans [...] The most seditious parts were always loudly applauded by the audience and [...] the play always attract[ed] larger audiences than any other." In addition, he noted that the informant had also pointed out the political implications of the venues and the producers who staged *Kichaka-Vadha*: "The play was specially selected for the Ganapati festival at Poona." Public celebrations devoted to the Hindu god Ganapati and to the seventeenth-century founder of the Maratha empire, Shivaji Maharaj, were an amalgam of religious-cultural-political events that Tilak had introduced to harness Hindu religious sentiment in the service of the nationalist agenda, as further discussed below. Morison built his case with additional details from secret police files maintained on playwright Khadilkar. Labeling Khadilkar "one of the most dangerous of the extremists," he

65 In this and the next paragraph all information and quotations come from Judicial Department Records, No. 503 of 1910; Letter No. C. 4-Confl., 14 January 1910; Maharashtra State Archives.

stressed that the Police Department's "Secret Abstract contains many references to him, among others an account of a most suspicious visit paid by him to Nepal." Focusing on the text of the play, Morison asserted, "It is an open secret in Poona, known to every school boy there, that Kichaka and his followers represent Lord Curzon and his subordinates in the administration of India." In a final argument he furnished thirteen selections from the dialogue as "samples of the innuendos that abound in the play" and that were "specially applauded at the performance at which [his] informant was present;" and he insisted that the informant was confident that "there could be not the remotest doubt that the audience applauded them as hits at the British Government of India." In less than two weeks Commissioner Morison's recommendation to prohibit all performances of *Kichaka-Vadha* was approved by a resolution of the Governor in Council dated 27 January 1910. Copies of the ban were sent to "all District Magistrates in the Presidency proper and to all Political Agents [...] and to the Inspector General of Police for insertion in the Police Gazette with sufficient explanation to enable the play to be identified."

Khadilkar and Other Playwrights' Strategies of Resistance

Given this environment of police surveillance, harassment and proscription, the vast majority of the nationalist plays employed allegory to circumvent anticipated government action or at least delay it for as long as possible.[66] Although colonial authorities slowly decoded the political message in these plays and eventually banned production and publication, the authors' allegorical strategies – at the minimum – bought enough time to propagate their ideas of cultural and political resistance for varying periods of time and, on occasion, to successfully defend themselves against the routine charges of sedition.

Some playwrights, like Anant Vaman Barve, Gopal Govind Soman and D.V. Nevalkar, turned to abstract allegorical characters, places and events. Thus in Barve's play *Lokmat Vijaya* (Triumph of Public Opinion, 1898) fictional characters signified contemporary personalities: Vicharswatantraya (Liberty of Thought) represented Tilak; Deshabhiman (National Pride) represented D.A. Khare, another nationalist figure; Ektantra (Absolute Authority) represented the British Secretary of State for India; Unmad (Madness) represented Poona's Special Plague Officer W. C. Rand who had been recently assassinated for polluting Hindu sacred places during a plague outbreak; and Raktapata (Bloodshed) represented Damodar Hari Chapekar who had been hanged for Rand's murder on the basis of a confession

66 Given this tendency in colonial drama and other genres – in India and elsewhere – one can understand, although not agree with, Frederic Jameson's assertion that all "third-world texts [...] necessarily project a political dimension in the form of national allegory" in "Third-World Literature in the Era of Multinational Capitalism," 69. See Aijaz Ahmad "Jameson's Rhetoric of Otherness and 'National Allegory,'" 3–25, for a systematic rebuttal of Jameson's thesis.

Bhaubandki (Family Feud, 1909)

gained by threats and subterfuge.[67] Place names followed a similar pattern: Swetpuri (Land of the Whites) meant England, and Arya Mandal (Land of the Aryas) meant India. Additional hints in the plot and characterization reinforced contemporary parallels: Vicharswatantraya, for example, was made a proprietor of a printing press to resemble Tilak who owned several publications. A memorandum by the Oriental Translator to Government, dated 2 May 1899, analyzed Barve's allegory in *Lokmat Vijaya* and ruled that "the aim of the author seems to be to inculcate the doctrine that sovereign power (Rajasatta) should be controlled by the voice of the people (Lokmata) in India and not entrusted to a bureaucrat in England invested with absolute authority (Ektantra)." The Oriental Translator also recognized that Barve had purposefully altered some details, in order "to render the similitude inexact and thus leave a loophole of escape for the writer in the event of his being charged with any offence." In another of Barve's strategies, some lines even hinted that granting freedom to the people of India would win their loyalty to the British Crown. But such stratagems did not work. The Oriental Translator concluded: "While glorifying Tilak as the embodiment of liberty of thought, the writer attributes all kinds of unworthy motives to the Secretary of State for India, who is accused of trying to suppress public opinion and to bring

67 All material on Barve and *Lokmat Vijaya* in this paragraph comes from Judicial Department Records, Vol. 167 of 1899, Maharashtra State Archives, Bombay.

its exponent Tilak into trouble." This was considered sufficient reason to declare the play as falling within the "category of objectionable and libelous writings unfit to be brought upon a stage." Abstract allegorical characters were similarly utilized to signify contemporary political figures and events by Nevalkar in his musical play *Dandadhari* (Power to Punish, 1909) and by Soman in his musical drama *Bandhavimochan* (Liberation from Foreign Yoke, 1898) staged by the Arya Subodh Natak Mandali (Aryan Enlightenment Theatre Company) at the Ripon Theatre on Grant Road in Bombay.

Other playwrights, however, cloaked their political allegories behind thicker cultural camouflage. They claimed simply to be celebrating their Indian heritage, that is, dramatizing events from the nation's folklore, history or religious epics. Two plays – Anna Martand Joshi's seven-act musical drama *Shiv Chhatrapati Vijaya* and Ramchandra Mahadeo Mhaiskar's *Vijaya Torna* – turned to the exploits and exhortations of Maratha martial heroes against Muslim rulers of India, a potent strategy since Hindu audiences typically saw that fight as analogous to the one against the British. In keeping with that approach Khadilkar's highly popular play *Bhaubandki* (Family Feud, 1909) depicted the court of the celebrated Peshwas, just as had the very first Marathi prose play, Kirtane's *Thorle Madhavrao Peshwe*, five decades earlier. In *Bhaubandki* Khadilkar deployed Ramshastri Prabhune, a fiery judge from a period of Maratha history when the Peshwa dynasty was threatened by infighting and disorder. Ramshastri's passionate arguments for unity among the Marathas echoed Tilak's appeals for accord between the two tussling factions of the nationalist party. Although *Bhaubandki* was banned for a period in Poona, the prohibition was rescinded on appeal. Two other plays – Shankar Sitaram Chitnis' *Khara Rajput* (True Rajput, 1898) and Vasudeo Rangnath Shirvalkar and Vinayak Trimbak Modak's *Rana Bhimdeo* (King Bhimdeo, 1892 and 1908) – capitalized on the heroic feats of Rajput warriors, whose battles against Muslim rule, like those of the Maratha warriors, symbolized the campaign against the British.

The remaining allegorical plays – Kane's *Drauni Mani Haran*, Dikshit's *Kalicha Narad* (Troublemaker Narad, 1910), and, above all, Khadilkar's *Kichaka-Vadha* – mined the *Mahabharata*, the massive repository of ancient narratives that has shaped India's religious beliefs, philosophy, law, literature, art and performance.[68] Thus these playwrights chose material that could be claimed as absolutely unimpeachable, namely, one of the founding texts of Indian culture. The dramatists utilized the *Mahabharata* also because the audience was intimately familiar with the epic's plots and personalities and was thus alert to their accumulated meanings, associations and resonances. Such coded sources facilitated subtle, indirect, and surreptitious communication. Just as importantly, to the audience the *Mahabharata* was at once history, legend, myth, and religious text, and so it not only loved and but also

68 Although the *Mahabharata* may have originated in the eighth or ninth century B.C.E., the epic as it now exists was most probably compiled in 400 B.C.E., and successive reciters poetspriests added material until circa C.E. 400.

revered many of its major characters.[69] Given such an attitude, the playwright of the Indian resistance could count on their heroic characters' veiled political exhortations to carry nearly religious sanction and urgency. Not accidentally, these stories, then as now, also guaranteed crowded theatres. Finally, in the context of the independence movement, simply by depicting India's heroic past, the dramatists inspired patriotism, encouraged participation in the freedom struggle, and offered an antidote to spreading cultural colonization.[70]

Comments in the newspaper *Pragati* (Progress) – extracted in the Judicial Department's Confidential "Report on Native Papers for the month ending July 16, 1910" – illustrate how some of these playwrights utilized *Mahabharata* stories to call for anticolonial political action. With its pro-British leanings, *Pragati* warned that Dikshit's production of *Kalicha Narad*, staged in Kolhapur by the Rashtriya Natak Mandali (National Theatre Company), may appear to be a "quite harmless" adaptation of the *Mahabharata* but in fact harbored "an allegory of a harmful character [...] calculated to do immense mischief."[71] It pointed out that Dikshit's depiction of the character Krishna who in the *Mahabharata* was "forced to do wrong involuntarily bears a great resemblance to Lord Morley." This was an accurate reading because Secretary of State for India John Morley had "reluctantly sanctioned" two Acts of Parliament aimed against the Indian National Congress' Extremist wing, maintained good terms with the leader of its rival Moderate wing, and favored granting independence to India.[72] Other *Pragati* observations showed how Dikshit had selected and modified *Mahabharata* characters and events to make them emblematic of contemporary figures and developments. The arrogant villain Galava who heaps scorn and abuse on his subordinates personified the typical British official, and his servant who smilingly endures kicks and insults from Galava but himself perpetrates outrageous injustice on his own subordinates typified petty Indian officials in the colonial machinery. Similarly, Subhadra's plea to her noble husband, Arjuna, to punish their evil monarch reflected the call for revolutionary action by the Indian National Congress' Extremist wing, and Kunti's appeals to her son Bhima, the epic's mighty warrior, to avenge her honor, represented *Hind Mata*, or Mother India, beckoning her sons to war against foreign

69 Such categories, in any case, are Western demarcations, which the Indian audience consider immaterial. Audiences in India commonly pay as much homage to divine abstractions as to their physical or virtual manifestations, whether in the temple, theatre, cinema or drawing room.

70 During this period, for analogous reasons, though not propelled by the same allegorical and political schemes, a number of Indian writers in other genres and languages also turned to adapting stories from Hindu religious texts.

71 All quotations from *Pragati* in this paragraph are from "Report on Native Papers for the month ending July 16, 1910," Judicial Department Confidential Compilation No. 2083, File No. 192 of 1910, Maharashtra State Archives, Bombay.

72 Smith, 772, 764; another historian describes Morley as "the most sympathetic British friend India ever had in the highest post of imperial power," Wolpert, *A New History of India*, 280–281.

oppression. Predictably, the government imposed a ban on the staging of *Kalicha Narad*, according to a Judicial Department resolution dated 26 October 1910.[73]

Kichaka-Vadha: The *Mahabharata* as Nationalist Theatre

Khadilkar's *Kichaka-Vadha* stands as the most sensational, politically compelling and popular anticolonial play of the period. On the surface it appeared to be simply an adaptation of *Mahabharata* stories for the theatrical pleasure of a Hindu audience.[74] In reality, however, *Kichaka-Vadha* was a powerful insurgent drama crafted to demonstrate – through allegory, allusion and implication – the effectiveness of the radical methods advocated by the Extremist wing of the Indian National Congress and, conversely, the futility of the cautious approach espoused by its Moderate wing for forcing the British out of India. The debate about means was a momentous one among Indian nationalists at the time, and only a few months after *Kichaka-Vadha* opened in Poona this dispute led to the historic split within the Indian National Congress at the raucous Surat Session in 1907. The crucial difference between the two wings represented two divergent but main streams of opinion.[75] The Liberals or National Liberals led by Gopal Krishna Gokhale – generally dubbed the Moderates – advocated working within British colonial law, i.e., using exclusively constitutional and peaceful means. On the opposite side, the Nationalists or Nationalist Revolutionaries led by Lokamanya Tilak and Aurobindo Ghosh – generally called the Extremists – opposed perpetuating British jurisdiction at any cost and insisted on using all available means, including unconstitutional and direct or violent action.[76]

In *Kichaka-Vadha* Khadilkar turned to the *Virata-Parvan* or the *Book of Virata* in the *Mahabharata* to champion the position of the Extremist wing at this time of intense crisis in the nationalist movement.[77] In the Sanskrit original the five noble Pandava brothers and their common wife, Draupadi, come to King Virata's capital to spend their thirteenth year of exile, as dictated by the terms of their loss at a rigged game of dice in which they forfeited their realm. During this final year they must remain incognito in order to reclaim their kingdom from their victorious cousins, the Kauravas of Hastinapura; if they fail, they will be forced into a forest exile for another twelve years. Disguised as royal retainers, they spend their time in

73 Judicial Department Government Resolution, No. 6144, dated 26 October 1910, Maharashtra State Archives, Bombay.

74 Historically, a number of Indian genres, including traditional theatre and dance forms, have explored the story of Kichaka's attempted rape of Draupadi.

75 For a succinct overview of this conflict, see Crane, 56–79.

76 Kulke and Rothermund 278–82; Spear 771–2, Wolpert, *A New History of India*, 277, 279–81. A decade later, Mahatma Gandhi reconciled the two approaches through his middle course of *Satyagraha* or peaceful non-cooperation, i.e., unconstitutional but non-violent action, and Khadilkar, as noted above, embraced *Satyagraha* and wrote new plays like *Menaka* and *Savitri* espousing Gandhian ideals.

77 *Mahabharata. Vol. III: Book 4: The Book of Virata; Book 5: The Book of the Effort.*

Vidyaharan (Knowledge Seized, 1913)

the employ of King Virata and perform a host of services in his court, household and beyond. The Commander of Virata's army, Kichaka, notices Draupadi and begins to pursue her incessantly; her five husbands, however, cannot intervene because of their need to maintain their disguise. In a covert scheme Draupadi offers Kichaka a night-time rendezvous in the dancing hall, where Bhima, lying in wait, kills him in secret without compromising the Pandavas' disguise.

With a strategic selection of events from the *Virata-Parvan*, new dramatic action, several invented secondary characters, and fresh dialogue in place of the epic's long poetic narrations and direct addresses, Khadilkar's *Kichaka-Vadha* embodied a political allegory in which key elements cohered in an extended system of double meaning to refer subtly but clearly to parallel developments in British India in the early years of this century. In this overall scheme, the heroic Pandavas' unjust and temporary servitude echoed the Indians' subjugation under colonial rule, Kichaka's molestation of the chaste and beautiful Sairandhri (Draupadi in disguise) represented the British viceroy's abuse of Mother India, the excessive caution of Kankabhatta (Yudhisthira in disguise) resembled the Moderate faction's ineffectual constitutional approach, and the success of Ballabha (Bhima in disguise) signified the efficacy of the Extremist faction's radical approach.

In order to concentrate attention on those narrative details that best served his allegory, Khadilkar eschewed the *Mahabharata*'s initial episodes about the Pandavas' arrival, their arrangements for employment and their varied activities in the service of the king. Instead he began his play a full ten months into the *Virata Parvan* narrative – on the day that Kichaka first lays eyes on the beautiful Sairandhri and instantly desires to possess her. So from the start, the playwright clearly framed the central issue in terms of the attempted molestation of an innocent woman by an unscrupulous warlord, emphasizing the political parallel of the rape of a nation by an occupying force headed by Lord Curzon, the detested British viceroy from 1899 to 1905. Besides deleting most of the *Mahabharata*'s expository material, Khadilkar also excised several episodes because they did not serve his political objectives. Thus he eliminated the fascinating stories of Kichaka's followers trying to set fire to Draupadi on his funeral pyre, Bhima's merciless massacre of Kichaka's kinsmen, the Kuru army's rout at the hands of the Pandava brother Arjuna dressed in female garb, the Virata Crown Prince's hilarious flight from battle, the Pandavas' defeat of the Trigarta army, and the marriage of Arjuna's son and Virata's daughter.

On the other hand, where needed by his overall strategy, Khadilkar invented details to emphasize parallels in early twentieth-century India. For example, to parody Viceroy Curzon's frequent pique in dealings with his own government in Britain, Khadilkar's Kichaka, without any precedent in the *Mahabharata*, threatens to leave the Kingdom of Virata with his followers unless he gets his way with Sairandhri. Historian Sarvepalli Gopal has documented how Lord Curzon "laid down lines of policy and took crucial decisions, while the home government [...] acquiesced;" whenever there was reluctance from Whitehall in London, he threatened to resign and leave with his key officials.[78] According to Leonard Mosley's biography of the powerful viceroy, Curzon "felt himself strong enough, and far enough away, to act alone, and if need be, in defiance of Westminster."[79] In a mock exaggeration of Curzon's warnings to the British Prime Minister, Kichaka threatens to depose King Virata: "You know well that this throne of yours that my might keeps steady I can overthrow in less than a second."

In order to further the nationalists' argument that a weak Prime Minister in Britain had allowed excessive power to the viceroy in India, Khadilkar enlarged the *Mahabharata* king's one-sentence refusal to intervene against Kichaka into a new extended court scene, where Sairandhri pleads in vain for the king's protection, just as the nationalists had futilely sought the intervention of successive prime ministers in London. In the scene Kankabhatta warns Virata of the consequences of his inaction, "When orphan women are arbitrarily raped and an oppressed populace endures its days in meek silence, and yet the ruler does not wake up and discharge his duty, then the foundation of *dharma* that undergirds a ruler's throne will weaken and before long his kingdom will be destroyed."[80] Despite Sairandhri's supplication and Kankabhatta's appeal to dharma, Virata vacillates and equivocates,

78 Gopal, 222.

79 Mosley, 79.

80 In its broadly understood usage *dharma* means law, duty, faith. *Dharma's* immense semantic field is apparent in M. Monier-Williams' list of more than two hundred meanings in his *Sanskrit–English Dictionary*.

"I understand, but [...] humans are born with a sense of dharma as much as a sense of self-interest: although I am a king, I am also human."The scene concludes with Virata washing his hands of Sairandhri by expelling her to a forest temple outside his city, "Sairandhri, I have saved your honor in this durbar. But it is not politically prudent for me to make Kichaka Maharaja an enemy over a dasi like you." By making Virata turn a blind eye to Sairandhri's certain rape at the temple, Khadilkar stressed the moral culpability of weak Westminster governments, providing further justification for terminating their administration of India.

Khadilkar encapsulated the conflicting positions of the two nationalist camps in his Pandava characters' passionate speeches and actions as they engage in an analogous discussion about the right approach for defending Draupadi's honor. Deviating from the *Mahabharata*, where Yudhisthira and Bhima do not discuss Draupadi's plight with each other, Khadilkar created a series of debates – unfolding across the play's five acts – between Kankabhatta and Ballabha as well as between Kankabhatta and Sairandhri on how best to proceed in her defense. Reflecting the Moderate view that inopportune action could prolong British rule, Kankabhatta recommends patience and warns against hasty action: "Bhima, stay calm. At this time we must not get trapped in anger and do anything imprudent [...] That some heated action today might expose our disguise and force the delicate Draupadi back into exile is a thought I simply cannot stand." But Ballabha presents the Extremist view, "Maharaja, a war cannot be fought without cruelty and heartlessness." Sairandhri also articulates the Extremist position, "Towards an avowed enemy, why behave with justice and compassion? Maharaja, if we are compassionate towards a viper and let it escape, then tomorrow won't the responsibility for the deaths of those killed by that viper not fall on our heads?" Exercising his traditional prerogative as the first born, Kankabhatta, continues to overrule them, "Draupadi, Bhima, I am telling you again very clearly, put aside today's question about killing Kichaka [...] It's not that I will never give my permission; but methods other than killing have not yet been exhausted." Nonetheless by the end of the play, Ballabha and Sairandhri succeed in convincing Yudhisthira to sanction the use of force against Kichaka.

Kichaka-Vadha: Hinduism, History and Rightful Violence

In order to rally mass support for anticolonial resistance, leaders of the Extremist wing, preeminently Tilak, had strategically fused patriotism with recently reformulated ideals of a resurgent Hinduism. They roused Indians to defend Mother India as well as Hinduism, which they used synonymously with Indianness as manifested in the nation's predominant cultural and religious institutions, values, and mores. Echoing this double appeal of Hindu nationalism, Ballabha contends that even though the Pandavas have never hated Kichaka and his kinsmen or hindered their happiness, "Kichaka wants to kidnap our source of happiness, our treasure – this noble and pious Draupadi – and rape her. Without fear of god or dharma, he arrogantly indulges in all sinful pleasures just as he wishes." This potent combination recurs in Sairandhri's urgings as well, "Kichaka persecutes poor defenseless people; and no matter how many times thoughtful men try to reason with him, he persists in this tyranny. Shouldn't we remove from his hands the instrument of his tyranny – his depraved body? Is this not the sacred duty of everyone devoted to dharma?" Sairandhri's words, in fact, echoed Tilak's speech given at the 1897 Shivaji Coronation Festival and published in *Kesari*, where he argued that the Hindu religious text *Bhagavadgita* did not fault a person for killing someone if the act was motivated by unselfish and benevolent aims. The Maratha hero Shivaji's killing of the Mughal general Afzal Khan to liberate the Hindu populace from Muslim tyranny was often held up as an illustration of this point by Tilak as well as other Extremist leaders like Aurobindo Ghose and Bipin Pal and the India House militants operating from London.[81] Sairandhri's argument, moreover, mirrored the Extremists' view that since the Moderates' strategy of reasoned persuasion had failed, rightful violent action became the only alternative, a point that is reiterated in the play's final moment as Ballabha strikes his fatal blow.

Kichaka, representing the hated Viceroy Curzon, lives up to his sinful portrait. When his wife, Ratnaprabha, falls at his feet in the crowded court and intercedes on Sairandhri's behalf in the name of her own *pativrata*, a Hindu wife's vow of devotion to her husband, Kichaka thunders, "Sairandhri, the pativratas of the past won't protect you; the pativratas of the future won't protect you; and the pativrata of the present won't protect you." He then declares, "This Kichaka has the power to tear apart the shackle of marriage clamped to his leg – with a kick like this and drag away Sairandhri," as he aims a kick at Ratnaprabha and lunges towards Sairandhri. Kichaka's attack on another man's wife alluded to Curzon's attempted rape of another man's land, while Kichaka's public betrayal of his virtuous wife signified Curzon's betrayal of his own nation's ideals of liberal democracy. Not only did Curzon oppose democracy for Indians, he "did not even [...] believe in democracy and equality for his fellow country-men in Britain," according to biographer Mosley.[82] Kichaka goes so far as to defy Bhairava, Shiva's awe-inspiring manifestation and the temple deity where Sairandhri is banished: "I regard this Bhairava as the servant who washes my bed linens and cleans my pot of spit [...] Nobody in this world can equal me. I am the foremost, and then there are the all the other gods." Just as Kichaka's mockery of his own cultural and religious principles justified violent action against him, Curzon's betrayal of his national creed warranted the violent overthrow of his rule.

In other details as well, Khadilkar's Kichaka resembled Viceroy Curzon, who "was bursting with vanity and ambition," and notorious for his imperiousness and scathing tongue.[83] Even a sympathetic historian like Vincent Smith noted

81 Chakrabarty and Majumdar, 72–4.

82 Mosley, 87.

83 Gopal, 224.

Vidyaharan (Knowledge Seized, 1913)

"the overbearing manner, the brusque speech, the cutting comment," the delight in "pomp and power," the "pedagogic hectoring," and the "romantic and imperialistic" nature of "one of the least loved" viceroys – all aspects shrewdly captured, albeit with mock exaggeration, in Khadilkar's portrait of Kichaka.[84] The tenor of Kichaka's bombast, "I can force Indra out of heaven, drag Indrani close to me and sit on the throne of heaven itself" and "I am the god of gods. I am the king of kings" is not too different from some of Curzon's boastful declarations. Curzon described his official tour of the provinces and princely states in 1900 as "my triumphal march through India."[85] Kichaka's extended preening during his ceremonial welcome by Virata, which opens the play and immediately establishes the parallel between him and the Viceroy, mirrored the extravagant Delhi Coronation Durbar of 1903 that Curzon had organized primarily to parade himself in princely pomp and which he proclaimed as "the greatest series of shows that have been seen for hundreds of years in Asia."[86]

Curzon's self-regard was matched only by his contempt for those he governed. Claiming that the British were in the country working "for the good of India,"

84 Smith, 751, 753–5.

85 Quoted in Mosley, 86.

86 Quoted in Gopal, 252. The durbar, of course, was meant to celebrate the coronation of King Edward VII, but Curzon often referred to the event as "our Durbar." Some newspapers at the time dubbed it a "Curzonation" and a *Tamasha* or meaningless spectacle.

he told a gathering of his compatriots in Calcutta, "I believe in [...] the capacity of our own race to guide [India] to goals that it has never hitherto attained."[87] Curzon called himself "an Imperialist heart and soul," dubbed the nationalists' plea for self-rule as mere "vapourings of a few misguided idealists," and scoffed, the "Congress is tottering to its fall [...] and one of my ambitions while in India is to assist it to a peaceful demise."[88] In his biography David Gilmour notes that when Curzon was asked "why he did not appoint a native to his Council, he replied, absurdly, that in the entire country there was not an Indian fit for the post."[89] Many of Kichaka's insults hurled at the blameless Sairandhri reminded the audience of Curzon's impertinent and humiliating comments about India. At the Calcutta University Convocation of 1900 Curzon had declared, "I am struck by the extent to which, within less than 50 years, the science and the learning of the Western world have entered into and penetrated the Oriental mind, teaching it independence of judgment and liberty of thought, and familiarising it with conceptions of politics, and law, and society to which it had for centuries been a complete stranger."[90] "The highest ideal of truth," he announced five years later at another convocation of the same institution, "is to a large extent a Western conception."[91] Kichaka's remark, "These dasas and dasis need to be kicked every now and then [...] Kick them while getting up, shove them while sitting down; if we don't treat them like this, they think they are the equals of us Kichakas and Anu-Kichakas, they resent our grandeur, and they find our reign oppressive," resembled Curzon's comment that Congress leaders were being presumptuous in seeking equality and self-rule. Other characters' comments about Kichaka also parallel contemporary pronouncements about the viceroy. In 1904 Dinshaw Wacha, the former president of the Indian National Congress, had referred to him as that "exalted python who has been so viciously doing mischief all round."[92] Thus when Sairandhri compares Kichaka to a deadly viper that must not be allowed to get away, the audience would have quickly grasped the contemptuous allusion to Curzon.

In keeping with his overall thrust Khadilkar chose a sacred temple as the location for *Kichaka-Vadha's* final climactic events, so that the Extremist wing's call for just violence against British rule could be imbued with Hindu religious fervor and sanction. The original *Mahabharata* story's setting – a dance hall where Arjuna disguised as a transvestite gives dancing lessons during the day and where Bhima hides in the shadows to ambush Kichaka at night – provided neither the religious resonance for the punishment of a sinful Kichaka, nor suited the tastes of his largely modern bourgeois Hindu audience. In Khadilkar's new setting his

87 Quoted in Mosley, 88.

88 Quoted in Gopal, 225 and Mosley, 88, 87.

89 Gilmour, 168.

90 Curzon, 243.

91 Curzon, 360.

92 Quoted in Gopal, 298, note 488.

avenging nationalist hero, Ballabha, assumes the role of a Hindu deity both literally and figuratively: unbeknownst to the other characters and the audience, Ballabha removes the life-size statue of god Bhairava in the eponymous temple and stands motionless in its place. In a coup de théâtre, when a frenzied Kichaka pursues Sairandhri into the temple and raises his hand to break the "statue," the deity himself appears to seize Kichaka's hand – to the amazement of Kichaka and Sairandhri as well as the audience. Ballabha offers Kichaka one last chance to desist and escape with his life but is met with more insults and defiance. With a single strike to the chest, Khadilkar's god-like nationalist hero kills Kichaka with supreme ease – in contrast to the *Mahabharata*'s prolonged combat between equally matched antagonists – presaging both the efficacy of the Extremists' methods and the successful attainment of their ultimate goal.

Kichaka-Vadha: Impact and Achievement

The power of Khadilkar's anticolonial allegory was evident in *Kichaka-Vadha's* immense popularity throughout the Deccan. By the beginning of 1910 the *Times* in London acknowledged the play's wide appeal, "A most pernicious influence has been exerted by a play acted all over the Deccan, as well as in Bombay city, to crowded houses."[93] The paper fumed that Khadilkar "has written several plays, and in all of them may be found sneers at and depreciation of the British rule, but in *Kichaka-Vadda*, or *The Killing of Kichaka*, he has surpassed himself." It continued, "No Englishman who has seen the play" would ever forget "the tense scowling faces of the men as they watch Kichaka's outrageous acts, the glistening eyes of the Brahmin ladies as they listen to Draupadi's entreaties, their scorn of Yudhisthira's tameness, their admiration of Bhima's passionate protests, and the deep hum of satisfaction which approves the slaughter of the tyrant."[94] Its imperialist bias aside, the *Times'* description of the audience reaction testified to the success of Khadilkar's political and theatrical strategies.

The *Times* article asserted that productions of *Kichaka-Vadha* may in fact have led to actual violent attacks on colonial officials: "Nor are signs lacking that the teaching of the play is bearing fruit." The *Times* linked the play to two recent sensational events, including the murder of the Collector of Nasik as he was entering the Vijayanand Theatre: "Within two years of its first appearance, and in the same Presidency, an attempt is made to assassinate Kichaka's successor, Lord Minto. And it is in a native theatre which has seen *Kichaka-Vadd* acted that

93 "A Seditious Drama of the Deccan," *Times*, 18 January 1910, 5. All quotations from the *Times* in this paragraph and the next are from this date. The article was reprinted in the *Times of India* (5 February 1910) and the *Bombay Gazette* (7 February 1910); incidentally, this reprinting in quick succession has led to occasional mix-ups in the dates and publications cited for this article in some later Marathi- as well as English-language scholarship.

94 This language again reminds us of the race factor noted in the "nigger Othello" letter in the *Calcutta Star* sixty years earlier.

Mr. Jackson is murdered."[95] Describing *Kichaka-Vadha* as "abounding in every form of incitement to an emotional audience," the *Times* demanded the government ban the play. To justify its call for censorship of the stage, something it did not endorse in Britain, the *Times* rationalized, "A theory evolved in the West may not fit in with the facts of the East."

Well before the British press called for the suppression of *Kichaka-Vadha*, the imperial police and bureaucracy were already, as described earlier, developing police files on the playwright, conducting undercover surveillance of performances in Bombay and Poona, and building a case for banning the play. But prior to its eventual proscription in 1910, Khadilkar's *Kichaka-Vadha* – like the other Marathi plays at the turn of the century – had already *performed* the idea of successful nationalist resistance and the idea of the end of imperial dominion – on the public stage and thus, inevitably, on the political stage of colonial India. Given the range and power of the police, legal and administrative machinery of suppression arrayed against them, theirs was no small achievement, because, as Edward Said argued in *Culture and Imperialism*, just as "the enterprise of empire depends upon the *idea* of *having an empire*," decolonization depends upon the idea of the *end* of empire posited by the anticolonial artist.[96]

Bibliography

Ahmad, Aijaz. "Jameson's Rhetoric of Otherness and 'National Allegory.'" *Social Text* 17 (1987): 3–25.

Bayly, Christopher. "Liberalism at Large: Mazzini and Nineteenth-century Indian Thought." In *Giuseppe Mazzini and the Globalization of Democratic Nationalism, 1830–1920*, edited by Christopher Bayly and Eugenio F. Biagini, 355–74. Oxford: Oxford University Press, 2008.

Bengal Hurkaru and India Gazette. 12 August 1848; 19 August 1848.

Bharucha, Rustom. *Rehearsals of Revolution: The Political Theatre of Bengal*. Honolulu: University of Hawaii Press, 1983.

Booth, Michael R. *Theatre in the Victorian Age*. Cambridge: Cambridge University Press, 1991.

Brown, Donald M. *The Nationalist Movement: Indian Political Thought from Ranade to Bhave*. Berkeley: University of California Press, 1961.

Calcutta Gazette. 5 November 1795; 10 March 1796; 16 March 1796.

Calcutta Star, 20 August 1848.

Chakrabarty, Dipesh and Rochona Majumdar, "Gandhi's *Gita* and Politics as Such." In *Political Thought in Action: The Bhagavad Gita and Modern India*, edited by Shruti Kapila and Faisal Devji, 66–87. Cambridge: Cambridge University Press, 2013.

Chatterjee, Sudipto. *The Colonial Staged: Theatre in Colonial Calcutta*. Calcutta: Seagull Books, 2008.

95 For the name of the theatre, I draw on Wolpert, *Tilak and Gokhale*, 230.

96 Said, *Culture and Imperialism*, 11.

Crane, Robert I. "The Nature of the Rift within the Indiana National Congress, 1893–1910." In *The Congress and Indian Nationalism: Historical Perspectives*, edited by John L. Hill, 56–79. London: Curzon Press, 1991.
Curzon, George Nathaniel. *Notable Speeches of Lord Curzon*. Edited by C. S. Raghunatha Rao. Madras: Arya Press, 1905.
Das Gupta, Hemendra Nath. *The Indian Stage*. 4 vols. Calcutta: Metropolitan, 1934–1946.
Desai, Vasant Shantaram. "Years of Glory: 1880–1920." In *The Marathi Theatre*, no editor, 9–40. Bombay: Popular Prakashan, 1963.
Deshpande, Kusumwati and M.V. Rajadhyaksha. *A History of Marathi Literature*. New Delhi: Sahitya Akademi, 1988.
Fay, Eliza. *Original Letters from India*. London: Hogarth, 1986.
Fischer-Lichte, Erika, Josephine Riley and Michael Gissenwehrer, eds. *The Dramatic Touch of Difference: Theatre, Own and Foreign*. Tubingen: Gunter Narr Verlag, 1990.
Frith, Nicola. "Rebel or Revolutionary? Representing Nana Sahib and the Bibighar Massacre in English- and French-Language Texts and Images." *Interventions: International Journal of Postcolonial Studies* 12, no. 3 (2010): 368–82.
Frost, Christine Mangala. "30 Rupees for Shakespeare: A Consideration of Imperial Theatre in India." *Modern Drama* 35 (1992): 90–100.
Gänzl, Kurt. *William B. Gill: From the Goldfields to Broadway*. London: Routledge, 2002.
Gargi, Balwant. *Theatre in India*. New York: Theatre Arts Books, 1962.
Gilmour, David. *Curzon: Imperial Statesman*. New York: Farrar, Straus and Giroux, 2003.
Gokhale, Shanta. *Playwright at the Centre: Marathi Drama from 1843 to the Present*. Calcutta: Seagull Books, 2000.
Gopal, Sarvepalli. *British Policy in India 1858–1905*. Cambridge South Asian Studies. Cambridge: Cambridge University Press, 1965.
Guha, Ranajit. "'Neel Darpan:' The Image of the Peasant Revolt in a Liberal Mirror." *Journal of Peasant Studies* 2, no. 1 (1974): 1–46.
Guha-Thakurta, P. *The Bengali Drama: Its Origin and Development*. 1930. Westport: Greenwood, 1974.
Halsband, Robert. "The First English Version of Marivaux's "Le Jeu de l'amour et du hazard." *Modern Philology* 79, no. 1 (1981): 16–23.
Hansen, Kathryn. *Stages of Life: Indian Theatre Autobiographies*. London: Anthem Press, 2011.
Hopkins, A. J., ed. *Globalization in World History*. New York: Norton, 2002.
India. *A Collection of the Acts Passed by the Governor General of India in Council in the Year 1910*. Calcutta: Superintendent Government Printing, India, 1911.
______. *The Unrepealed General Acts of the Governor General in Council*. Government Legislative Department. 2 vols. Calcutta: Government of India, 1958.
Jameson, Fredric. "Third-World Literature in the Era of Multinational Capitalism." *Social Text* 15 (1986): 65–88.
Judicial Department Records. Maharashtra State Archives, Bombay.
Kulke, Hermann, and Dietmar Rothermund. *A History of India*, 2nd ed. London: Routledge, 1990.
Kundu, Manujendra. "The Dramatic Performances Act of 1876: Reactions of the Bengali Establishment to Its Introduction." *History and Sociology of South Asia* 7, no. 1 (2013): 79–93.
Lebedev, Gerasim Steppanovich. *A Grammar of the Pure and Mixed East Indian Dialects*. London, 1801.

London Chronicle. 10–13 December 1774.

Loomba, Ania. *Gender, Race, Renaissance Drama*. Delhi: Oxford University Press, 1992.

Mahabharata. Vol. III: Book 4: The Book of Virata; Book 5: The Book of the Effort, trans. van Buitenen. Chicago: University of Chicago Press, 1978.

Marathi Theatre. No editor. Bombay: Popular Prakashan, 1963.

"Messink, Barnard" and "Messink, James." In Highfill, Philip H., Kalman A. Burnim and Edward A. Langhans. *A Biographical Dictionary of Actors, Actresses, Musicians, Dancers, Managers, and Other Stage Personnel in London, 1660–1800*. 14 vols. to date. Carbondale: Southern Illinois University Press, 1978–.

Monier-Williams, M. *Sanskrit–English Dictionary* Delhi: Munshiram Manoharlal, 1976.

Mookerjee's Magazine. New Series 5, nos. 36–40 (1876).

Mosley, Leonard. *Curzon: The End of an Epoch*. London: Longmans, Green, 1961.

Mukherjee, Sushil Kumar. *The Story of the Calcutta Theatres: 1753–1980*. Calcutta: K. P. Bagchi, 1982.

Nair, P. Thankappan. "Lebedeff's Life in Calcutta." In Saha, ed., *A Grammar of the Pure and Mixed East Indian Dialects*, i–xxii.

Popple, William. *The Double Deceit: or, A Cure for Jealousy: A Comedy, as It Is Acted at the Theatre-Royal, in Covent-Garden*. London: T. Woodward, 1736.

Raha, Kironmoy. *Bengali Theatre*. New Delhi: National Book Trust, 1978; 2nd rev. ed. 1993.

Rangacharya, Adya. *The Indian Theatre*. New Delhi: National Book Trust, 1971.

Report on Native Newspapers (January–June 1876), Bengal Presidency. National Archives, New Delhi.

Saha, Mahadev Prasad. "Gerasim Steppanovich Lebedev." In Saha, *A Grammar of the Pure and Mixed East Indian Dialects*, xxix–lxii.

Saha, Mahadev Prasad, ed. *A Grammar of the Pure and Mixed East Indian Dialects: By Herasim Lebedeff*. 1st ed. 1963, 2nd ed. Calcutta: Firma KLM, 1988.

Said, Edward. *Culture and Imperialism*. New York: Alfred Knopf, 1993.

Seal, Anil. *The Emergence of Indian Nationalism: Competition and Collaboration in the Later Nineteenth Century*. Cambridge: Cambridge University Press, 1971.

Sen, Sailendra Nath. *History of Freedom Movement in India (1857–1947)*; 4th ed. New Delhi: New Age International, 2009.

Singh, Jyotsna. "Different Shakespeares: The Bard in Colonial/Postcolonial India." *Theatre Journal* 41 (1989): 445–58.

Smith, Vincent A. *The Oxford History of India*. Ed. Percival Spear. 4th ed. New Delhi: Oxford University Press, 1981.

Solomon, Rakesh H. "Towards a Genealogy of Indian Theatre Historiography." In *Modern Indian Theatre: A Reader*, edited by Nandi Bhatia, 3–30. New Delhi: Oxford University Press, 2009.

Spear, Percival. *A History of India*, vol. 2. Baltimore: Penguin, 1965.

Theatre. "Theatre Legislation in India." 20 February 1877, 41.

Times. "A Seditious Drama of the Deccan." 18 January 1910.

Times of India. "Drama of the Deccan." 5 February 1910.

______. "*Navakal* editor jailed." 16 July 2003.

______. "Rane 'Supporters' Attack Marathi Daily Office over Editorial." 22 January 2009.

Torri, Michelguglielmo. "'Westernized Middle Class,' Intellectuals and Society in Late Colonial India." In *The Congress and Indian Nationalism: Historical Perspectives*, ed. John L. Hill, 18–55. London: Curzon Press, 1991.

Viswanathan, Gauri. *Masks of Conquest: Literary Study and British Rule in India*. New York: Columbia University Press, 1989.

Wolpert, Stanley A. *A New History of India*. 6th ed. New York: Oxford University Press, 2000.

______. *Tilak and Gokhale: Revolution and Reform in the Making of Modern India*. Berkeley and Los Angeles: University of California Press, 1961.

Yajnik, R. K. *The Indian Theatre: Its Origins and Its Later Developments under European Influence*. London: George Allen & Unwin, 1933.

Part II

Kichaka-Vadha,
or
The Slaying of Kichaka

Krishnaji Prabhakar Khadilkar

Translated by
Rakesh H. Solomon

A NOTE ON THE TRANSLATION

My paramount concern while making this translation has been to strive for utmost fidelity to the original text of *Kichaka-Vadha* and to recreate in English some of the flow and flavor of the play's dialogue. To this end, I have sought, among other things, to preserve the rhetorical trajectory of the Marathi dialogue. Thus, to the extent feasible in English without linguistic infelicity, my text tries to reproduce, within sentences and speeches, the order in which the original Marathi script imparts information to an audience from moment to moment. Through this reconstructed structure, the translation seeks to replicate – as well as highlight – Khadilkar's dramaturgic strategies for generating dramatic irony, ambiguity, comedy, misunderstanding, tension, and surprise. Such elements predominate in the play, emerging organically from its central device of double identities. Throughout the translation, moreover, I have tried to convey the directness and simplicity of Khadilkar's dialogue – qualities that powered his ability to sway vast audiences in the cause of nationalist resistance. The degree to which this translation achieves its goals, of course, will be for others to judge.

To keep the need for consulting a glossary to a minimum, I have incorporated within the translation itself equivalents or close approximations of many Marathi and Sanskrit terms. At the same time, however, in order to capture the vital linguistic and cultural flavor of the original dialogue, I have also left untranslated a number of Marathi and Sanskrit terms that the characters employ with some frequency. These include unique terms for Hindu rituals, ceremonies and concepts as well as terms used repeatedly to address family members, elders, superiors, or royalty. In a couple of cases, moreover, I have retained original terms because adequate translations would have been unwieldy or simply impossible in spoken English. All original Marathi and Sanskrit terms have been italicized at their first occurrence and brief explicatory notes have been provided in a separate section of key terms.

In the translation that follows I have eschewed notes about historical figures and events alluded to in the text, since my discussion in Part I provides both the broad contours of the play's historical context and many minute details of the allegorical framework that drives the action and enriches the work's political import and resonance.

Overall, I have kept several audiences in mind: general readers, undergraduate as well as graduate students, and scholars of theatre, literature, history, and culture. I have assumed, moreover, that actors and directors, especially at colleges and universities, may also use this translation and that they will necessarily modify the text to suit their particular theatrical aesthetic and audience needs.

LIST OF CHARACTERS

(in order of appearance)

Saudamini	*Maid to Sudeshana*
Sairandhri	*Draupadi disguised as maid to Sudeshana*
Mandahasini	*Maid to Sudeshana*
Sudeshana	*Wife of Virata and sister of Kichaka*
Ratnaprabha	*Wife of Kichaka and sister of Virata*
Virata	*Maharaja of Matsyadesha*
Kichaka	*Commander of Virata's army*
Maitreya	*Old Priest*
Kankabhatta	*Yudhisthira disguised as a courtier at Virata's court*
Ballabha	*Bhima disguised as principal chef of Virata's kitchens*
Siddhapaka	*Cook*
Vidyadhara	*Student*
Prathama Dasi	*First Maid*
Dvitiya Dasi	*Second Maid*
Guru	*Teacher and Scholar*
Purohit	*Priest*
Chanchala	*Maid*
Chapala	*Maid*

ACT ONE

Scene 1

Place: Main entrance to the royal palace. Enter: Saudamini and Sairandhri.

SAUDAMINI

Oh, Sairandhri, have you ever seen so much fun in Hastinapura or Indraprastha as you are seeing here today? My Matsyapuri is really special! I have seen many cities but none matches even a tiny alley here.

SAIRANDHRI

But, Saudamini, will you let others talk, or will you do all the talking?

SAUDAMINI

Maybe your Indraprastha is as big as Matsyapuri – or maybe it's twice as big, four times, eight times, or even sixteen times as big. But does Indraprastha have men as brave and handsome like those in my city?

SAIRANDHRI

Saudamini, can't you speak a bit softly? Shshsh! What if someone hears us discussing men? Women should not discuss men's physical appearance – only their virtues.

SAUDAMINI

What are we *dasis* going to do with men's virtues? Don't tell me tales like an old woman. And tell me one thing, you also spend a lot of time with Ballabha *aachari* – is that only because he cooks well, or is it because he has grown big and strong by gorging from the kitchens? Why are you so quiet now, Sairandhri? Please don't feel angry. But don't men praise women's looks? The moment two or three loafers sit down to chat, don't they say awful things about the looks and makeup of other peoples' wives, as if their own wives are the loyal ones around and other men's wives are not?

SAIRANDHRI

Why should we do what men do?

SAUDAMINI

Then should dasis go about acting like dignified *bai sahebs*? Actually, I would like to behave like a bai saheb, but I can't unless I become one myself. I am not like you. You are a dasi but act like a bai saheb. And today when there is a gathering of such gorgeous men in Matsyapuri, my tongue begins to wag freely! All the good-looking men of Matsyapuri are roaming the streets of the city showing off their finery and their handsome faces and trying to charm women – and yet I should remain quiet! How's that possible? And see, today is the day for all the fine-looking men of the city to crowd along the streets majestically because Matsyapuri's most handsome man, Kichaka Maharaja, will be entering the royal palace with great pomp and ceremony. Sairandhri, you haven't seen Kichaka Maharaja yet, right?

SAIRANDHRI

Before our Bai Saheb appointed me to this job he had gone from here.

SAUDAMINI

You've been in this job for, what, ten months now? Before you arrived Kichaka Maharaja had left for Hastinapura. He lived there for eight months in great style as the honored guest of the Kauravas, and he struck a lasting friendship with Duryodhana Maharaja, the Lord of the Kauravas. Kichaka Maharaja is returning today, and Matsyapuri is filled with celebrations – it is laughing and dancing with joy! But, Sairandhri, I want to know why you have this gloomy look?

SAIRANDHRI

I don't like to perform *aartis*, *ovalanis* and such rituals for anyone other than family. So I had begged Rani Saheb to take me off my assignment for today's ceremony at the great gates of the palace. Rani Saheb had agreed to my request, but who knows why her order has changed again!

SAUDAMINI

And that's a problem! I deliberately asked Rani Saheb to give you this assignment. You don't know, but Kichaka Maharaja is a hundred times more handsome than your Ballabha aachari or Kankabhatta! You won't find another man with his divine looks anywhere in the world. I am absolutely sure. If we don't go ahead and perform the aarti and greet him today, when will we ever get a chance to get so close to this handsome man? I have done you such a big favor. Because I didn't get them this assignment, Mandahasini, Sashimukhi, Kamala, and Chapala were all cursing me.

SAIRANDHRI

What for?

SAUDAMINI

Because I sidelined them and recommended you.

SAIRANDHRI

It would have been better if you had not done me such a favor.

SAUDAMINI

Once you catch a glimpse of Kichaka Maharaja – experience a *darshana*, a vision, of this beautiful idol – you'll be grateful to me all your life. If you merely stand near him and let your eyes feast on him, you'll feel that your life has been worthwhile.

(Mandahasini enters)

MANDAHASINI

Oh, Saudamini, I think Rani Saheb is about to arrive. Ratnaprabha Bai Saheb is coming with her. Is everything ready for the aarti and ovalani?

SAUDAMINI

This great one has come to supervise my work! Who told you to come here? I am well aware that Rani Saheb is coming. Go, go sit there! You don't need to show your face to the men here! Go, go there and join those sitting on the ground there waiting for Rani Saheb and Kichaka Maharaja to arrive.

MANDAHASINI

Rani Saheb told me, "Go and get things ready there;" so I came! Otherwise, I am not interested in talking to you.

SAUDAMINI

Look at these; see the preparations; inspect everything carefully! Here's the *kalash* with holy water; here's the box of *kumkum*; here are the twigs from a mango tree; here's the *toran* of green leaves on the palace's main doors. Except for performing Kichaka Maharaja's ovalani, nothing is left to be done. We – both of us – are standing here, alive and awake, with all the items needed for the aarti and ovalani. Open your eyes wide and look. Satisfied? Isn't everything ready? Now go, go!

(Mandahasini starts to leave)

SAIRANDHRI

Mandahasini, you know how to perform aarti, so why don't you come stand here? I will go and take the spot near Rani Saheb.

(Mandahasini seems to return)

SAUDAMINI

Go, go! Go back to your own work. Your mouth may be watering to work here, but I won't let you.

(Mandahasini leaves)

Sairandhri, when this Mandahasini is so ugly, how can she even think of showing her face to men?

SAIRANDHRI

But if she takes my place here, how's that a problem for you?

SAUDAMINI

I will never take her with me. Twice or thrice she came with me to the temple. But seeing her pitch-black forehead, not one damned man even glanced towards us! I swear, not one man looked at us. But when you are with me or when I'm alone, forget the shameless men; even the great scholar, the famous, or the devout one will turn towards us again and again! Like vultures eyeing a piece of meat! Rani Saheb's entourage has arrived! Let's light the oil lamps!

(Rani Sudeshana, Ratnaprabha, and Mandahasini enter)

SUDESHANA

Saudamini and Sairandhri, have you lit the lamps and prepared everything for the ovalani?

SAUDAMINI

Yes, Bai Saheb, everything is ready. We are just waiting for Kichaka Maharaja.

SUDESHANA

Yes, *Dada* will be here right now; a horn has sounded, and their procession seems to be here already.

MANDAHASINI

Yes, Bai Saheb, Virata Maharaja and Kichaka Maharaja just stepped down from their chariot and sought blessings from the venerable Guru Purohit. Their procession has entered the palace courtyard and is approaching.

SAUDAMINI

(Aside to Sairandhri)

What a bitch Mandahasini has been? Before everyone else, she went and saw Kichaka Maharaja! Did you see that?

SUDESHANA

Mandahasini, where is Ratnaprabha Saheb?

MANDAHASINI

Bai Saheb, she's right here.

SUDESHANA

Oh, *Vahini*, why are you standing back like this? Until now you were so eager to see Dada, but now when Dada has been awarded the title of Maharaja and is approaching us, you seem so hesitant! Really, Vahini, that my dada Kichaka Maharaja's wife would feel embarrassed to greet him and shower him with flowers is astonishing!

RATNAPRABHA

Vahini, at this moment of joy why is my heart feeling strangely uneasy? I will certainly welcome him and garland his neck, but what if he does not look at me?

SUDESHANA

Shshsh, why do you countenance such doubts in your heart, Vahini?

(Moving closer to her)

Dada was surely away in Hastinapura for eight or nine months, but could his love for his paramount rani ever decrease?

RATNAPRABHA

The women of Hastinapura are supposed to be incredibly beautiful.

SUDESHANA

A man more handsome than my dada you won't find in this world, nor, Vahini, a woman as beautiful as you.

RATNAPRABHA

Vahini, why are you needlessly mocking me like this?

SAUDAMINI

Really, Bai Saheb, I know the women of the North are extremely beautiful. My own mother is from the North.

MANDHASINI

That's why you look like such a born beauty!

SAUDAMINI

Stop blathering! And may I speak frankly, Bai Saheb? The men of the North are dull and boring. But those here in the Deccan are so magnificent. It's no surprise why Kichaka Maharaja was treated so well by everyone there. Look at this Sairandhri here who served the Pandava Rani Draupadi. She is so beautiful – like a heavenly constellation! But not so the men with her: Chef Ballabha and Kankabhatta's faces are so damned dull that you can't even bear to look at them!

SAIRANDHRI

Oh dear Saudamini, a momentary flash of lightning is praised by people, but if that lightning continues, its terrifying thunder makes the same people hate it!

RATNAPRABHA

Indeed, Vahini, your new dasi is really very beautiful. Her voice is so soft and sweet. If all the women of Hastinapura are like her, no woman of Matsyadesha should let her husband even cast a glance towards her.

Offstage: Sounds of trumpets. Cheers of "Hail to Kichaka Maharaja!" Enter: Virata, shaded by a royal ceremonial parasol; Kichaka, also under a ceremonial parasol and accompanied by two young women carrying ceremonial whisks; Kankabhatta; Maitreya; and various others. Petals shower down on Kichaka from above. All toss gulal and flowers on Kichaka. More shouts of "Hail to Kichaka Maharaja," etc.

VIRATA

Kichaka Maharaja, your arrival has made my city of Matsyapuri very happy, and your dear *akka* is waiting here eagerly to greet you. Next to her stands your rani, and my sister, Ratnaprabha. Speak a few words of greetings to them, and please enter the royal palace.

KICHAKA

Akka, seeing you all so eager to greet me makes me most happy. In Hastinapura I was greeted with great pomp and ceremony, and Duryodhana, the Leader of the Kauravas, showed me immense respect; but that happiness, Akka, cannot compare with the joy I feel today. Because for mankind love is an entirely special and wonderful thing. Are you all well?

SUDESHANA

Dada, naturally Matsyapuri is so happy to know that you were shown such great respect at Hastinapura. We are all very eager to hear of the ways in which you were honored by Duryodhana, and my vahini Ratnaprabha is waiting most anxiously to hear directly from your mouth about all your exploits. Let's go into the royal palace without any delay!

KICHAKA

Akka, once I convey Emperor Duryodhana's message to Virata Maharaja in the *durbar*, I will tell you about all my exploits; but how much Emperor of the World Duryodhana respects me should be evident to anyone who simply looks at these garments of mine. All of you already know that Duryodhana as Monarch of India has bestowed upon me the title of Maharaja of Matsyadesha. Our Virata Maharaja has been bestowed the new title of Emperor of Matsyadesha by the Monarch, and I have been instructed to continue my former duties and responsibilities now as Maharaja under our Emperor Virata. But Akka, and Emperor of Matsyadesha Virata Maharaja, I tell you that I don't think true honor was bestowed upon me by the title of Maharaja. Real honor, I believe, has been conferred upon me by these magnificent clothes. Look at this royal parasol that the Emperor of the World Duryodhana gave me when awarding me the title of Maharaja of Matsyadesha! Does anyone here know whom this grand parasol originally belonged to? Maitreya, could you read the initials on this parasol and tell us the name of the former owner?

MAITREYA

Whose initials could I possibly find on this parasol! Some journeyman tailor who stitched the umbrella might have sewn two or three of his own initials on it! Or perhaps some illustrator who drew the pictures might have hidden his initials among these images of women he has drawn!

KICHAKA

Maitreya, you have no understanding of matters of state!

MAITREYA

I have left all tedious matters to this Kankabhatta here. Earlier I used to be responsible for all matters of state…

KICHAKA

But what made you do that?

MAITREYA

Once this Kankabhatta came here from the durbar of Yudhisthira Maharaja, I transferred all matters of state to him. According to Yudhisthira he is highly skilled in matters of state.

KICHAKA

If this Kankabhatta is from Yudhisthira's durbar then just like him he too will squander all his wealth and his wife in gambling, and clutch all his brothers and sink into the pit of misery!

MAITREYA

He has no brothers or anyone else. Judging by how we treat each other, I could be considered his brother: I take care of him, and he keeps to himself! As regards his wealth, early on he possessed just one leaky tumbler. Now with his gambling he has won a few pennies. A real smart fellow! I see no signs of a wife whatsoever, and yet none of the money he wins in gambling ever remains with him!

KICHAKA

You used to be with Yudhisthira. Do you know to whom this royal parasol once belonged? Do you recognize it?

KANKABHATTA

Looks like it's from Indraprastha.

KICHAKA

Do you know whose it is?

KANKABHATTA

It is Yudhisthira Maharaja's.

KICHAKA

What? Why such a cranky voice? Every man in Matsyapuri should be thrilled that I have been bequeathed this royal parasol. Leader of the Matsyas Emperor Virata Maharaja, before presenting these clothes to me, Emperor Duryodhana Maharaja was most impressed by my expertise in archery and mace fighting. Had I grown up in Hastinapura, Uncle Shakuni would not have needed to sneak around rigging the game of dice! Just one blow from my mace would have pulverized Bhima's thighs! Had I been present at Draupadi's *swayamvara* ceremony, she would have become my rani! My absence at those events drove Duryodhana Maharaja to tears, as he told me.

VIRATA

Kichaka Maharaja, your exploits are truly glorious.

SUDESHANA

Indeed, Dada, had you been present in Hastinapur, Draupadi would not have needed to marry five husbands.

RATNAPRABHA

You possess the virtues of all five Pandavas put together. That you were not present at Draupadi's swayamvara is my great good fortune!

KICHAKA

And had I been present, Draupadi would have been brought here to your palace as your dasi. Today I promise and declare that soon when the Kauravas and Pandavas go to war, with these arms I will show Bhishma, Drona, Karna, and others my great feats of valor. After I kill Bhima with my mace and take Arjuna's life with my arrows, I will grab Yudhisthira by his hair and drag him to my feet. I will then pardon him and bestow upon him the gift of life but make him wear a Brahmin beggar's rags and dispatch him to the forest for a life of penance. The remaining Pandavas, the twins Nakula and Sahdeva, will be forced to wear women's clothes and toss flower petals on me. That I will demonstrate such amazing acts of heroism is a promise I have made to Emperor of India Duryodhana. For showing him such exploits against the Maharaja of Indraprastha, Duryodhana has promised to reward me at the end of the war with the Pandavas' wife Draupadi. So, Akka, please tell your Vahini that the day when Draupadi will become her dasi is not too distant!

MAITREYA

But let's hope that does not happen. Because compared to Ratnaprabha Rani Saheb, Draupadi is far more beautiful.

RATNAPRABHA

A rani turns into a dasi, and a dasi into a rani – such a day can never come!

Kichaka-Vadha (The Slaying of Kichaka, 1907)

KICHAKA

The rani will remain a rani. As for the rest, my actions will make that day come! To remind me of my resolution, the Lord of the Kauravas has inscribed the word "Bhima" on my left ankle. When a blow from my mace knocks Bhima to the ground, I will squeeze the life out of him with my left toe. When my arrow throws Arjuna off his chariot, my right foot will kick his forehead. And so the name "Arjuna" has been inscribed on my right ankle. And Akka, tell your Vahini, after Draupadi's swayamvara, her father, Maharaja Drupada, had presented the five Pandavas with five diamond rings with the words "Draupadi's Husbands" carved on them. The Kauravas won these rings from them in the game of dice, and because I will destroy the Pandavas in the approaching war and become Draupadi's sole husband, the Kauravas put these five rings on the five fingers of this brave, this fortunate and powerful hand! After putting these rings on my fingers, the Kauravas hailed me in the crowded durbar with shouts of "Draupadi's Husband!" "Draupadi's Husband!" *(The dasis with ceremonial whisks accompanying Kichaka exclaim, "Hail to Draupadi's Husband Kichaka Maharaja!")* Virata Maharaja, Akka, these dasis with the royal whisks are gifts to me from the Emperor of the World and Monarch of India. To perpetually remind me of my promise to crush the Pandavas, I have commanded them to always hail me with the words, "Draupadi's Husband!"

(The two dasis shout, "Draupadi's Husband Kichaka Maharaja!" The other dasis, except Sairandhri, shower petals on him)

SUDESHANA

(To Saudamini and Sairandhri)

Now light the oil lamps and perform the ovalani.

(Saudamini performs the ovalani. Sairandhri, with ovalani vessels in her trembling hands, freezes in place)

KICHAKA

Akka, it looks like you have such beautiful dasis that they can put the dasis of Hastinapura to shame. The first time I entered Emperor of India Duryodhana's royal temple, one thousand lovely young dasis stood holding ovalanis for me. The Lord of the Kauravas entreated me to take some dasis I liked back to Matsyadesha. To honor the Emperor of India's request, I brought these two jewels from the land of Gandhara to stay in my natakashala. Duryodhana Maharaja will soon be coming here in his search for the Pandavas, and I want to present him some pretty dasis. I was worried as to where I would find them. But, Akka, seeing this Sairandhri of yours who can even put a lamp's radiance to shame, I am not worried anymore. If you don't mind, Akka, will you give this Sairandhri to me? Virata Maharaja, will it be a problem for you if this dasi is no longer in your natakashala?

VIRATA

Oh no, not at all. She is never with me.

KICHAKA

And, Akka, there are so many other dasis to serve you. Duryodhana Maharaja will be coming here to Matsyadesha and staying in my natakashala. Sairandhri can live with me, and I will teach her how to please valiant men and present her to Emperor of India Duryodhana.

MAITREYA

Only Kichaka Maharaja is worried about taking good care of the Emperor of India.

RATNAPRABHA

(To herself)

It is said that if men spend too much time abroad, their hearts go astray; and it looks like that's not a false adage.

SAUDAMINI

Sairandhri, I have already carried out my *drishti* duties. Why are you still waiting to perform Maharaja's ovalani? Maharaja has done you the honor of keeping you in his special natakashala, so don't you get so lost!

(Aside to Sairandhri)

Don't forget to be grateful to me for this favor I am doing you today!

(Back to everyone)

Maharaja has honored my friend so unexpectedly that she is feeling a bit bewildered. When a poor woman suddenly receives a kingdom's wealth, that's what happens for a moment or two. Please forgive me, but instead of my friend I will perform the ovalani.

KICHAKA

Akka, how could you appoint such a gorgeous fairy as a servant? That really amazes me! Such beautiful flowers deserve to be placed on the palms of one's hand and their fragrance inhaled with love, or else such flowers should be worn as adornment in one's hair. Does anyone ever trample them under one's feet!

(Saudamini performs the ovalani. Shouts of "Hail to Kichaka Maharaja" and "Hail to Draupadi's Husband, Kichaka Maharaja." More petals are showered on him)

VIRATA

Let us now enter the royal temple.

(More petals and gulal are tossed in the air. Still more cries of "Hail to Kichaka Maharaja," etc. All, except Maitreya and Kankabhatta, exit)

MAITREYA

Why, Kankabhatta, why has your face changed so totally? Why are you looking so downcast? You are shedding tears because your prey Sairandhri has escaped from your hands and has now landed in Kichaka's natakashala! Such dasi-courtesans are bound to be unfaithful! No matter how much of your gambling money you spend on them, they are never satisfied, not even a little!

KANKABHATTA

Why this unnecessary and senseless mockery?

MAITREYA

But, Kankabhatta, you are a poor Brahmin, and Sairandhri has received the honor of joining Kichaka Maharaja's natakashala. So why should you be gloomy? You should think of this loss as if you had lost a few pennies while gambling in Virata's court. In fact, now that Sairandhri has gone to Kichaka Maharaja, your expenses will become less. Always keep an eye on your expenses! What's the point in earning if you spend it all?

KANKABHATTA

What are you insinuating? I talk to her because we are both from the same village. I will never commit the terrible sin of eyeing a dasi.

MAITREYA

You had thrown a net and caught a fish which Kichaka Maharaja has now taken away. You should be relieved that you won't be committing a terrible sin after all. Everybody has now gone ahead, let's go and join them.

KANKABHATTA

You go on. I want to first convey Maharaja's orders to Chef Ballabha. I will get to the durbar just as they all reach there.

MAITREYA

Saudamini was saying that from time to time Sairandhri whispers in Chef Ballabha's ears, and from time to time she whispers in yours – so that is why you and Ballabha don't get along too well! Now that Sairandhri has a third man, I think the two of you will become friends!

KANKABHATTA

Maitreya, I want to ask you something about Kichaka Maharaja.

MAITREYA

When you were with Sairandhri, did you ever confide in me? I may be a bit old, but I am not dim. I am not getting trapped.

(Goes)

KANKABHATTA

(To himself)

Curse the day this Dharmaraja was born! Twelve or thirteen years ago I lost all my wealth in a game of dice and saw my own wife being humiliated by wicked people. And today I saw my own royal parasol being affronted and the reputation of my brothers being mocked by an arrogant and pompous snob – such misfortune has befallen me. Just because he has never encountered a man of matching strength who would teach him a lesson, this Commander of the Matsyadesha army kept pronouncing himself "Draupadi's Husband," "Draupadi's Husband!" – right before my eyes and while standing in front of Draupadi herself. Could the Pandavas' situation get any more appalling than this? Duryodhana, you were so incensed by Draupadi's womanly laughter at you during the *Rajasuya yajna* that you tried to strip her in public and exiled us into the forest. Has that not quenched your thirst for revenge? O Supreme God, when Duhshasana put his hand on Draupadi, you showed us a miracle by putting a bit of sense in the blind Dhritarashtra's heart and thus saving the Pandavas' honor. In the same way instill some sense into Maharaja Virata and Maharani Sudeshana and help the Pandavas get through this horrible situation.

(Leaves)

Scene 2

A road near the royal palace. Maitreya enters.

MAITREYA

Where has this Kankabhatta gone? Since yesterday the fellow's head has not been right. Saudamini is coming this way. Let me see what I can find out about Kankabhatta from her.

(Saudamini enters)

Saudamini, oh, Saudamini! You seem to be lost in your own world! Today's young girls have stopped looking at old men! In my days young girls were not like this. They would look at old men at least once. Oh, Lady Lightning! Oh, Lady Lightning!

SAUDAMINI

Greetings to you, Maitreya Bhattji. What is your command?

MAITREYA

Shall I bless you that you might have eight sons? Or daughters? Tell me how many do you want?

SAUDAMINI

I do not want a single child. Once a woman bears a child, men become bored with her.

MAITREYA

But we old men don't get bored.

SAUDAMINI

Why do you mention "old" men?

MAITREYA

OK! Instead of eight kids, shall I give you a blessing for eight husbands?

SAUDAMINI

What is this Bhattji? Just because I'm a dasi, you are making such fun of me! You should at least conduct yourself with the dignity of your advanced years.

MAITREYA

Old men and young men are the same when it comes to giving blessings. Besides, the more gray hair a man has, the more women give him respect because they consider him harmless. Except for you, no other dasi behaves so haughtily with me. All the other dasis talk to me, behave nicely with me …

SAUDAMINI

You think women look at you because they like your gray hair?

MAITREYA

Certainly, that's what I think.

SAUDAMINI

The only reason women don't avoid gray-haired men is that old men are a sure test of a woman's beauty. If even old men turn around and look slyly at a woman, then she can definitely wound the hearts of young men. So old man, why did you call out to me?

MAITREYA

Where is Sairandhri? She must have gone to live in Kichaka Maharaja's natakashala.

SAUDAMINI

No, she hasn't gone yet.

MAITREYA

What?! How can that be? No one in Matsyadesha dares disobey his word, and Sairandhri …

SAUDAMINI

That is very true. But Sairandhri did not consent. Yesterday, Sudeshana Rani Saheb did not insist that she go, but today …

MAITREYA

What happened today?

SAUDAMINI

The Anu-Kichakas, the followers and fellow caste-members of Kichaka Maharaja, have stuffed his head with the notion that Sudeshana Rani Saheb does not like the supremacy of Kichaka and the Anu-Kichakas in her husband's kingdom, and that she deliberately did not send Sairandhri in order to insult Kichaka. The prime minister has told the Rani Saheb that if she does not send Sairandhri right away, Kichaka Maharaja has made up his mind to openly affront the king and take away Sairandhri in the presence of everyone.

MAITREYA

So Sudeshana Rani Saheb must be all shaken up?

SAUDAMINI

What do you think?! Sudeshana Rani Saheb has gone to pacify Kichaka Maharaja.

MAITREYA

What is there to pacify?! Just send Sairandhri to him. Sairandhri is so beautiful …

SAUDAMINI

If an old Brahmin like you praises her, it's no surprise that Kichaka Maharaja is after her!

MAITREYA

I am not praising Sairandhri! This man here is not like Kankabhatta who gets entangled with dasis.

SAUDAMINI

Then why are you inquiring about Sairandhri?

MAITREYA

I was looking for Kankabhatta, so I have come to you to talk about Sairandhri!

SAUDAMINI

If you are trying to find Kankabhatta, why are you asking me about Sairandhri?

MAITREYA

This is how it is. Where there is Sairandhri, there must be Kankabhatta. If I try to search for him openly, I am not going to find his whereabouts that easily.

SAUDAMINI

Why?

MAITREYA

Because when men's secret affairs are exposed, it feels like a whack on the head; and in secret affairs even women try and dodge their neighbors as much as they can. So I think Kankabhatta will avoid my face, and Sairandhri will avoid yours. So let's do this: I will search for Sairandhri, and you look for Kankabhatta. Let's go!

(They leave)

Scene 3

Place: Temple of goddess Mahalaxmi. Kankabhatta, Ballabha and Sairandhri in conversation.

KANKABHATTA

Draupadi, we Pandavas are so mighty, but what use is it today? Other than recalling our magnificent past and bringing tears to our eyes, what can we do in our present situation? This Bhima destroyed Jarasandha with ease and can singlehandedly crush the entire Kaurava clan. Yet today we are forced to pretend as if Bhima is not here. Oh, Panchali, this Arjuna – who defeated all the Kauravas and their fellow maharajas at the time of your swayamvara, who conquered the entire earth, who rescued Duryodhana by defeating the Gandharvas, who compelled the Kauravas to lower their heads in front of you – today that great warrior Arjuna has to sit quietly wearing women's bangles! Until the almighty brings that day when we can show our bravery openly, I believe the best course of action is for us to swallow all our humiliations quietly.

SAIRANDHRI

Maharaja, you are an ocean of peaceful ideals, so it is natural for you to feel that all should calmly endure their oppressors' kicks. Setting aside the matter of how to act once our exile is over, now in our current exile in disguise, it seems you don't notice or understand other people's unhappiness. You get to sit in the durbar and engage in debates; Virata Maharaja seeks your opinion about truth and dharma; and during gambling matches he tosses a few pennies towards you. Content with this, the lord of the throne of Indraprastha asks his own wife to become another man's dasi – can anything more shameful than this happen to the Pandavas? "Spend a few days in slavery, and you begin to enjoy slavery." That is not how our progeny should remember the Pandavas' conduct in Matsyapuri; this is the only appeal this humble wife makes at the feet of her Maharaja.

KANKABHATTA

Draupadi, did I utter a single word to suggest that you go to Kichaka's natakashala?

SAIRANDHRI

Maharaja, yesterday had the Kauravas been present and heard Kichaka declare – in the presence of the Pandavas themselves – his resolve to make Draupadi join his natakashala, they would certainly have felt well rewarded for dispatching the Pandavas into exile. When the wicked Duhshasana pulled my sari in the Hastinapura durbar, you gripped your forehead and kept quiet because you accepted the reality that I was then a dasi won in a dicing match. But yesterday, I was not a slave, and neither were you.

KANKABHATTA

Draupadi, we are serving this period of exile in disguise; don't forget this.

SAIRANDHRI

That is why I say if the Kauravas see our condition today, they will burst with joy. Maharaja, I could endure not just twelve years' exile but even a lifelong exile. But this exile in disguise …

KANKABHATTA

Draupadi, once sins dislodge a person from his station, the punishment of exile is etched on his forehead. If he behaves properly in that exile, he wins the reward of an exile in disguise. If he spends those days of disguise with intelligence and righteousness, he will be restored to his original condition. This is the way life is.

SAIRANDHRI

Maharaja, when you were in exile, you didn't have to forget who you were, or what you were, in the past. Even in exile, the Pandavas used to amaze the world by their glory. But today what is your condition? You are the master of the throne of Indraprastha – but do you have the freedom to utter those words? When Jayadratha cast a sinful gaze at your wife, you captured him, humiliated him and made him a slave, and you spared his life only out of consideration for your sister. Just as you had done then, why didn't you come forward and show your might when

Kichaka-Vadha (The Slaying of Kichaka, 1907)

that evil animal Kichaka kept boasting and calling himself "Draupadi's Husband," "Draupadi's Husband?" Maharaja, I could endure even a lifetime exile, but this exile in disguise that steals one's virtues I cannot stand for even a second. During a physical exile, the body suffers; but during an exile in disguise, the mind suffers. The Pandavas' exile in disguise means that they agreed to forget their past greatness and live under the subjection of others. Maharaja, if a mind accustomed to freedom willingly spends two days in slavery, it quickly becomes weak and incapable of distinguishing between honor and dishonor; and, forgetting its former state of freedom, it begins to think it a virtue to put up with insults! If the Pandavas had gone to Hastinapura directly after their exile, the Kauravas would have found them frail in body but strong in mind, and all our enemies would have been afraid of us. But, Maharaja, greedy for crumbs of comfort thrown to palace servants, the Pandavas today are robust in body but feeble in spirit, and the Kauravas are happily clapping their hands in applause!

KANKABHATTA

Draupadi, you have to go to Kichaka's natakashala …

BALLABHA

Dada, how did you stay quiet when Kichaka declared he will keep Draupadi in his natakashala? If this Bhima had been present there, then just as I had sliced Jarasandha from head to toe and made one Jarasandha into two, I would have carved two Kichakas out of one. When Panchali told me about yesterday's events, I was more angry with you than with Kichaka. What can I say about that dreadful sinner, that awful animal Kichaka? But how did you tolerate the atrocious behavior of that outrageous man? Dada, when you saw your own royal parasol held above that animal's head and your blood did not boil with anger, that I think means the Pandavas are just not worthy of Indraprastha's royal parasol. While we Pandavas are alive, how can that charioteer's son Kichaka strut around as "Draupadi's husband?" Dada, shame on your righteousness and peaceful disposition!

KANKABHATTA

Bhima, stay calm. At this time we must not get trapped in anger and do anything imprudent. We are fortunate that you, Bhima, were not present at the event yesterday. That animal Kichaka can trample only on the letters of Bhima's name, but when the time comes, Bhima's kicks will smash that wicked man's forehead; that I can foresee clearly. But, Draupadi, today is not the time for anger. Bhima, that some heated action today might expose our disguise and force the delicate Draupadi back into exile is a thought I simply cannot stand. Just as clearly as I can see the present, I see the future ...

BALLABHA

But then what are you saying? That Draupadi should go to Kichaka's natakashala and defile her body? What's the point of getting back the throne of Indraprastha from the Kauravas in the future, if we have to endure such abusive oppression today? Dada, I am your younger brother, and I am feeling so ashamed at this that I would rather swallow flames and die! So after Kichaka sullies Draupadi, and when the whole world heaps contempt on us, does Yudhisthira Maharaja, by fulfilling his promise, want to ascend the throne of Indraprastha? Dada, people respect you for your reputation as *Ajatshatru*, the one who has no enemies, but he who does not rise in fury even when his wife is brutalized, shame on such an Ajatshatru!

KANKABHATTA

Bhima, will you listen to what I am saying? Today there is no reason for us to be so disturbed. The Pandavas are not used to living quietly under other people's rule, but when we accepted the condition of our exile in disguise, it was as if the Pandavas had happily volunteered to be ruled over by others. During such a situation, even in the face of atrocities it is not the best policy to act aggressively or openly. With eyes focused on our future prosperity, we should somehow pass these present uncomfortable days. Draupadi, don't be so miserable. No matter how much this arrogant braggart Kichaka carries on talking like this, I don't think the time will ever come for you to actually step into his natakashala. Maharaja Virata is wise and kind hearted, and Maharani Sudeshana's many virtues have earned her the affection of all her subjects. Draupadi, in our present situation mere verbal insults should simply be swallowed. But if that evil Kichaka wants to act on his words, then you appeal to Sudeshana, fall at her feet, rely on the truthfulness and nobility of the Maharani, and no harm will come to you from Kichaka.

(Curtain)

ACT TWO

Scene 1

Place: Courtyard of the royal temple. Rani Ratnaprabha, Maitreya and Mandahasini enter.

RATNAPRABHA

Oh, Maitreya Bhattji …

MAITREYA

At your command, Rani Saheb!

RATNAPRABHA

Where is he?

MAITREYA

Kichaka or Virata Maharaja?

RATNAPRABHA

The one who should be by my side!

MAITREYA

The one who should be by your side is on this side.

RATNAPRABHA

"This side" means?

MAITREYA

"This side" means "That side!"

RATNAPRABHA

I must tell Rani Sudeshana that her employees don't know how to talk.

MANDAHASINI

Maitreya Bhattji, Rani Saheb is asking you where has Kichaka Maharaja gone?

MAITREYA

That only dasis like you would know! When Kichaka Maharaja comes to the palace, he searches for Sairandhri or fools around with Saudamini or laughs with Mandahasini – so how am *I* to know? Besides Rani Saheb, when Kichaka Maharaja enters the royal temple all these dasis fly and hide like owls hiding from the sun. So we can't say where Kichaka Maharaja is or is not, nor where he will be or will not be!

RATNAPRABHA

Mandahasini, you walk a few steps ahead of us and find out whether or not he is in Sudeshana Vahini's palace!

MAITREYA

And as Kichaka Maharaja sets foot in Sudeshana Rani Saheb's palace, send me a signal immediately. Our Rani Saheb has planned a lunch for Virata Maharaja. And I have been ordered to attend. So what I mean to say is as soon as the food is served, call me.

(Mandahasini leaves)

RATNAPRABHA

Maitreya Bhattji, I want to ask you one question. Will you give me a straight answer – with a child's directness?

MAITREYA

I will give you an absolutely straight and childlike answer. How to talk with women in simple – facile – infantile language is child's play for me. Rani Saheb, as you are aware, earlier Maharaja had assigned me the task of teaching the ladies of the rani's household to read and write. Rani Saheb, you may ask me a question, and if you want a childlike answer with childlike gestures, I will give you that; if you want an answer in an adolescent's language, I can give you that, too; and I can even give you one in an old man's language. Because words, like prostitutes, follow me everywhere!

RATNAPRABHA

You are a learned and insightful *pundit* – so I am asking you. Give me the unvarnished truth. Is that dasi Sairandhri more beautiful than me?

MAITREYA

If Rani Saheb keeps her diamond and pearl jewelry with me, I'll give her my opinion.

RATNAPRABHA

Why's that?

MAITREYA

We are poor people. When we look at rich women, our eyes fall on their clothes and jewelry – not on their faces. Your jewels and Sairandhri's face are in my eyes!

RATNAPRABHA

OK, if Sairandhri wears these jewels, will she look prettier than me? Why is "he" interested in Sairandhri? Tell me the truth!

MAITREYA

Rani Saheb, what can I say? We men are such savants that even the ugly demoness Hidimba can please us! You must have heard how prince Bhima, despite having a great beauty like Draupadi as his wife, could not part from Hidimba. And, Rani Saheb, you should ponder this: if men were good judges of women's beauty, would women need to paint their faces and put on jewelry?

(Saudamini enters)

SAUDAMINI

Oh, Maitreya Bhattji, have you seen Sairandhri anywhere?

RATNAPRABHA

Saudamini, what is Vahini doing?

SAUDAMINI

Rani Saheb, she is waiting for you. Kichaka Maharaja's retinue has already arrived!

(Mandahasini enters)

MANDAHASINI

Rani Saheb, Maharaja is waiting for you.

RATNAPRABHA

Come on, Maitreya Bhattji, I too invite you.

(Mandahasini and Ratnaprabha leave. Maitreya starts to go)

SAUDAMINI

Oh, Maitreya Bhattji, will you wait for a while or not? Talk of food – and your old age disappears, and you leap like a youngster.

MAITREYA

What should I wait for?

SAUDAMINI

First tell me where is Sairandhri? Kichaka Maharaja has come and is ready to dine – and she has hidden her face!

MAITREYA

Is there a shortage of dasis to serve and fan him? If she has hidden her face, let her!

SAUDAMINI

But the Rani Saheb has asked me to find and bring her. This Sairandhri has no brains. It's a chance to join Kichaka Maharaja's natakashala, but is it in her fortune?

God proposes, but our action disposes! And I say, once she enters Kichaka Maharaja's natakashala – after the first, a second will also enter!

MAITREYA

But why are you searching for Sairandhri? Stupid girl! At today's lunch, instead of her you perform her serving duties – keep coming near Kichaka Maharaja as often as you can. You grasp this: Sairandhri has vanished somewhere – so you take advantage of it. Look, take some special dishes to serve him; come on, go. And serve me with particular care: I will praise you so much that Kichaka Maharaja will begin to want you.

SAUDAMINI

Today's special dishes have turned out very well! I will serve you till your belly bursts. How will you describe my beauty to Kichaka Maharaja, tell me?

MAITREYA

Your scrawny body, though filled with stale rotten mold obvious to any man's eyes, should to a man like Kichaka Maharaja appear as if it were the statue of a heavenly nymph.

SAUDAMINI

Beware! Such talk does not fill stomachs with meals!

MAITREYA

Though on this earth your dull face might look like a leper's, in heaven it will look like the moon. Though some scoundrels say that filthy saliva keeps dripping from your mouth, the touch of a lover will change that saliva into sacred water. I will prove this to Kichaka Maharaja.

SAUDAMINI

And understand, Bhattji, today's fruits have been picked from distant gardens! With this kind of talk, those will not come your way!

MAITREYA

Mischievous young men think your eyes look perpetually shut. But thoughtful men think your eyes hold arrows of beauty.

SAUDAMINI

Enough of teasing; let's go for the lunch. *(Holds his hand and pulls him away)* I will serve you so much food today that you will have to leave some in your plate.

MAITREYA

Even if you don't know how to win the hearts of young men, you have an old woman's expertise in holding the hand of an old man. From my present personal experience, I will recommend you to Kichaka Maharaja.

(They leave)

Scene 2

Virata and Kichaka are seated for lunch. Each is being fanned by a dasi. Kankabhatta and Maitreya are also seated. Sudeshana, Ratnaprabha, Mandahasini and Saudamini stand.

SUDESHANA

Ballabha, is everything ready?

(Ballabha enters from the kitchen)

BALLABHA

All done, Maharaja.

SUDESHANA

Are the special dishes prepared well? Today is your test. Kichaka Maharaja has just returned from Hastinapura. He should not find anything inferior here.

BALLABHA

Duryodhana Maharaja would sometimes come to Indraprastha to meet Yudhisthira Maharaja. I used to make similar food for him. And just as Duryodhana will remember my food for the rest of his life, so will Kichaka Maharaja!

SUDESHANA

Everything has been served. Dada should be invited to start.

VIRATA

Please begin, Kichaka Maharaja.

SUDESHANA

Maitreya Bhattji, you may start!

MAITREYA

Kankabhatta, what are you staring at?

SUDESHANA

What are you waiting for? Do start, Dada.

VIRATA

Begin, Maharaja.

KICHAKA

But where is she? For so long now, Akka, I have been telling you that I will not touch anything without her. Let her come.

SUDESHANA

Ratnaprabha Rani Saheb is standing right here! Dada, I didn't know you husband and wife are so fond of each other! Rani Saheb, please come stand next to Dada. Without you near him, not a morsel goes down my dada's gullet!

VIRATA

A husband's love for his wife should be like this. Bravo, Kichaka Maharaja! Bravo, Ratnaprabha Rani Saheb!

MAITREYA

Maharaja, hope you did not face similar difficulty while you were at Hastinapura.

KICHAKA

Emperor Virata Maharaja and Sudeshana Maharani Saheb, what makes you think I am waiting for her? Akka, for four days I have been asking you for your Sairandhri, but for four days now no one has cared to remember my wish! Remember, when my defeat of Trigarta was new, my wishes were fulfilled readily, even before I would mention them. Just because I was away from Matsyadesha for eight to ten months, has the value of my words gone down so much! Yesterday, Maharani Saheb, you had invited me to attend this lunch. I had insisted that I would attend only if Sairandhri would be present here as my dasi; otherwise, I would not attend. You had promised me, Maharani Saheb, that Sairandhri would be mine – that she would be my dasi at this lunch and that I could take her away with me after the meal. That promise, Maharani Saheb, came with your invitation.

SUDESHANA

Yes, I had given my word, and I will deliver Sairandhri to you after lunch.

KICHAKA

After lunch? The moment I stepped on this dais, Sairandhri should have been mine. Where is she? I will not touch anything unless I see her. Where is she? What? Won't come? Ten months ago I was never insulted like this in Matsyadesha. The minute I set foot on this dais Sairandhri would be mine – that was the promise yesterday, and today I am being served here by the lowly Ballabha! Go away – I will not eat food served by this common Ballabha *(pushes his plate away).*

VIRATA

What's this, Kichaka Maharaja? If she has committed any error, we'll think about it after the meal.

MAITREYA

Food once served should not be kicked.

KANKABHATT

Annam Bramheti Vyjanat! You cannot escape the curse that befalls him who kicks food.

KICHAKA

Shut up you wretches! What do you all know about how wealthy people live? You, who have to beg and entreat others for two helpings of food, are so thrilled when you get a piece of food that you place it on your head and dance – you were born only to eat. I not only have sumptuous food but all the things in the world that make life happy. So what are you praising food to me for? A man whose might creates rajas, maharajas and *adhirajas*; whose commands, as soon as uttered, compel legitimate rajas, maharajas and adhirajas to abdicate their thrones; whose power propels new kingdoms into prosperity and illustrious ones into oblivion; a man as brave as I should have all founts of pleasure lining up before me with folded hands and offering to serve me. Sudeshana, Maharani Saheb, I can force Indra out of heaven, drag Indrani close to me and sit on the throne of heaven itself. Only in order to respect ancient tradition, and because I had inadvertently called you Akka, I defeated Trigarta in battle and gave new life to the throne of Matsyadesha. Virata Maharaja and Sudeshana Maharani Saheb, I brought your kingdom back to you and applied the royal anointment on your foreheads. And just the other day I brought Virata Maharaja the title of Adhiraja from the Emperor of India. Thus I fulfilled all my promises – even if made inadvertently – and yet, I ask for a dasi, and you are reluctant to give her to me. Such stunning gratitude, such stunning gratitude! Akka, it's my wish – I tell you – rather, it's my order – Sairandhri should take this plate away and bring me another plate of food served with her soft hands, stand near me and fan me. Where is Sairandhri? Sairandhri? Won't come? I am leaving then!

SUDESHANA

Wait a little, I will send someone to call her. Sairandhri will come right away. Saudamini, where is Sairandhri? Ask her to come quickly.

SAUDAMINI

Ballabha has taken her to help him in the kitchen. In fact, I heard that many of these dishes were made by her.

KANKABHATTA

Many saints traveled great distances to Indraprastha just to taste food cooked by Sairandhri.

MAITREYA

These dishes seem to be so good that my mouth is watering. If not Sairandhri's, then even if Ballabha's creations enter my stomach, I won't complain.

RATNAPRABHA

I will take away your plate and get you another one.

KICHAKA

The greatness of your beautiful hands is in your palace. I am not your slave outside your palace.

RATNAPRABHA

The laws for women are the same everywhere. *(Picks up the plate)*

KICHAKA

Beware! The one who has been assigned the work should do it. Do you want to forfeit the respect given to a rani and be a dasi in a natakashala?

VIRATA

Sairandhri or whoever that dasi is – call her. For a minor matter, why are you fighting running battles?

BALLABHA

She is engrossed in work in the kitchen.

SUDESHANA

Saudamini, you go take her place and send her here.

SAUDAMINI

I was going there, but Ballabha wouldn't let me.

MAITREYA

Why Ballabha, son, what's it to you? What does it matter who does the chores – whether it's Sairandhri or it's Saudamini?

KANKABHATTA

If a skillful person assists you, food turns out better.

SUDESHANA

There are lots of servants. Ballabha, send Sairandhri out.

MAITREYA

Cooks behaving like stubborn rulers – how can this happen? Saudamini, you go to the kitchen! *(Begins to leave)*

BALLABHA

Turn back, you *shembedi*! Maharaja, if such dasis begin to cook, all the food will go bad – I cannot let her enter the kitchen.

SAUDAMINI

What shall I do, madam? If you order me, I will fan Kichaka Maharaja. *(Begins to fan him)*

KICHAKA

Go far away, shembedi! A pebble cannot replace a gem in a ring!

SAUDAMINI

(Moving away)

Men are donkeys! If we seek their affection, they kick us!

MAITREYA

Is this "Maharani" Sairandhri coming out, or do we have to go hungry today?

SUDESHANA

I will go myself and bring her – come Mandahasini, come along with me.

(Sudeshana and Mandahasini leave)

KICHAKA

Virata Maharaja, in your court women have become too stubborn! A mere dasi – and Sudeshana Rani Saheb has to go to get her! What stubborn women! I tell you clearly, this hide-and-seek of the Rani Saheb will not make me fade away in Matsyadesha. Until the time comes when you are capable of defeating Trigarta yourself, you cannot insult Kichaka and get away with it.

VIRATA

What strange ideas! Will we ever insult you? Sairandhri is a very good natured and thoughtful woman.

KANKABHATTA

And so Maharani is very fond of her.

SAIRANDHRI *(from within)*

I fall at your feet, spread my saree *pallava*, and beg – please save this unfortunate creature from the horrible cruelty of this mean beast.

KICHAKA *(stands up)*

Virata Maharaja, in your Matsyapuri and right in front of me, one dasi calls me a mean beast, and you all praise her for good behavior. I am amazed! Why *should* I be amazed? Rani Saheb, now I understand your actions! First, you sent Sairandhri away to insult me in front of everybody, and then you made that dasi abuse me by calling me a mean beast in the presence of all the servants to humiliate me still further. It is just with this goal that you had arranged the lunch! Enough, I am leaving. This Kichaka is not a fool who will wait until the dasi abuses him openly. Raja Virata, recall Matsyadesha's obligation to Kichaka before you encourage your wife's audacity. I am the one who made Virata's wobbly throne stable, and if it weren't for me, your Rani Saheb would now be a dasi in some Trigarta charioteer's natakashala.

VIRATA

What is this, Maharaja Kichaka! Needless suspicion! I will reassure you in just a short time …

KICHAKA

Raja Virata, keep in mind how enormous my might is. If I want I can drag any woman – not just from Matsyapuri but from anywhere in the world – to my natakashala. Raja Virata, consider the terrible consequence of one of your palace servants saying no to the valiant heart that has promised to take the mighty Pandavas' Draupadi to his natakashala. Enough, now I depart from here, but if within four days

Sairandhri does not come to live in my natakashala, then this day's insult ... Well, I will not use words anymore. Think what actions you must take.

(Exits)

VIRATA

What is this? So much anger! Such a small matter! Come, Maitreya, let's go and placate Kichaka Maharaja.

(Exits)

MAITREYA *(while leaving)*

All my astrological signs are bad today – why else was I so unfortunate that all I got was a mere glimpse at that plate of delicious foods? *(Exits)*

(Sudeshana brings Sairandhri out, holding her by the arm)

SAIRANDHRI

Bai Saheb, I fall at your feet – I entreat you by spreading my saree pallava – please do not surrender this unfortunate soul to that mean beast.

SUDESHANA

What is this? Sairandhri, you are merely a dasi – and because of you, Kichaka Maharaja was insulted and left in anger – do you think this is right? Vahini, you should have told him something! These dasis have become so arrogant. Such trash, but more haughty than you and me! Go, Sairandhri; go right now! Go to Kichaka Maharaja's palace; fall at his feet; bow your head in humility; fold your hands in supplication and say, "I have come to live in your natakashala."

SAIRANDHRI

Bai Saheb, if you are angry with me, then it would seem even God is angry with me. Bai Saheb, although misfortune has forced a virtuous woman like me to spend some time working as a servant for you, I am mindful of dharma, righteousness and good conduct. Bai Saheb, why do you wish to ruin your saintliness by asking me to do something that will break my *pativrata* – my vow of faithfulness to my husband? Your reputation for virtue, devotion to religion, and caring for orphans brought me here to serve you during my distress. When seeking your employment, I had fallen at your feet and entreated you never to ask me to do anything that would cause my husband to dislike me, nor to serve as a dasi to any man. And you had given me your word that you would protect my honor as if I were your younger sister.

SUDESHANA

Nothing doing. Sairandhri, you have to go to Kichaka Maharaja's natakashala this very moment.

SAIRANDHRI

You forgot your promise. But, Bai Saheb, I won't blame you – perhaps some great sin from my previous birth has caused this. How else is such an amazing change possible – you have turned from a saint-like lady into a cheap hussy?

KANKABHATTA

Sudeshana, Bai Saheb! Ratnaprabha, Rani Saheb! If in grief and anger Sairandhri has uttered an inappropriate word about Kichaka Maharaja or about you, please forgive her this time. What she means is that if, because of circumstances, a man as mighty as Kichaka Maharaja slips and falls into a net of impure desires and is inclined to indulge in a sin, then he can be brought back to his former virtuous

Kichaka-Vadha (The Slaying of Kichaka, 1907)

ways only by the efforts of a pious and righteous pativrata like you. Talk to him a little about dharma and reignite his righteousness so that it becomes as bright as it once used to be. This will bring blessings to pativratas like you.

SUDESHANA

Vahini, I am in a big quandary. I can't tell how Kichaka will react if I put in a word for a dasi. But, on the other hand, how can I ask Sairandhri to go to the natakashala against her will? Bai, please tell me!

SAIRANDHRI

Ratnaprabha Rani Saheb, Sudeshana Rani Saheb, you are both renowned in Matsyadesha for being great pativratas. I may be a poor woman in a terrible situation, but it is my desire to be like you in your great piety and virtue *(falls at their feet)*. Bai Saheb, think of me as if I were your orphan child. Ratnaprabha Rani Saheb, before judging my behavior as insulting to your husband, consider what if a situation like this were to befall Sudeshana Bai Saheb, who is a pativrata. How would her husband and your brother Virata Maharaja feel – how sad he would be – imagine that first. Sudeshana Bai Saheb, the order that you are giving this poor dasi, if the same order were to be given to Ratnaprabha Rani Saheb, as a pativrata she would be destroyed by grief – remember that. Only few women like you will understand why pativratas prefer to die than to have their pativrata broken. So I spread my pallava and beg. Don't see this as ordering a dasi, but rather see this as ordering a pativrata like yourself to join a natakashala. Please look upon me with kindness, the way one pativrata should regard another pativrata in distress. You are my owner; I am the slave; but forget that for a moment. Please do not destroy the moral center of one woman merely to save another woman's misplaced pride; do not set aside the ultimate dharma of all women. Protect this poor, righteous pativrata sister of yours.

SUDESHANA

Sairandhri, get up; don't mourn needlessly. You have fine qualities, and you are intelligent; I understand that. So I have tactfully disregarded the demand that Kichaka Maharaja has made from the very first day. But yesterday when I realized that he saw this as an insult, I gave him my word. Now this whole thing is acquiring a political dimension, and in politics men do not value virtue or good deeds, you know that.

KANKABHATTA

Politics and dharma ought to go hand in hand. Politics should not ride roughshod over righteous policy. To remind rulers of this principle, great women like you have been given the title of Maharani. If women don't control men's greed, the almighty Brahma's plan of creating women to regulate men's tendencies would appear to have been in vain.

SUDESHANA

Kankabhatta, I understand all these things, but I don't know how to act in this situation.

RATNAPRABHA

Maharani Saheb, I feel bad when I look at Sairandhri. If she were willing to do what *he* wants, I would not have objected to his wishes. And I would have been happy cursing the almighty for giving such beauty to a lowly creature rather than to a noble woman devoted to her pativrata. But seeing her moral strength, I feel like she is a sister to me. Sairandhri, don't grieve. We have four days' time – by then I will make him change his mind.

SUDESHANA

Ratnaprabha Rani Saheb, if you take it upon yourself, anything can happen.

(Curtain)

Scene 3

Place: A road.

Enter: Vidyadhara carrying a book of sacred writings under his arm, and Siddhapaka Achari holding a slotted spoon, a pair of tongs and some chewing tobacco that he crushes in his palm.

SIDDHAPAKA

Listen, Vidyadhara, come here, my boy, trying to avoid me; come here. Where are you rushing in such a hurry?

VIDYADHARA

Coming! Whatever you want me to do, tell me quickly. I have to go to Guruji's house right away.

SIDDHAPAKA

Yes, I know! But still, you don't have to go in such haste!

VIDYADHARA

Ugh! Keep some distance when you speak; you saw this sacred book and you sprinkled spit on it!

SIDDHAPAKA

(Shoots out a stream of spit)

It happens by mistake – it won't splash again.

VIDYADHARA

Most inauspicious! With such habits, how can you work as a cook, Siddhapaka?

SIDDHAPAKA

Listen, yesterday something funny happened! Kichaka Maharaja had a special lunch at the house of one of the Anu-Kichakas. While cooking a curry of fish chunks, my tobacco saliva drooled from my mouth straight into the curry pot! But Kichaka and the Anu-Kichakas just loved the curry and stuffed themselves like anything!

VIDYADHARA

Ugh, horribly inauspicious! Guruji was saying that the world's final degenerate era Kali Yuga is going to begin soon, and that may not be untrue.

SIDDHAPAKA

I too feel exactly the same. Yesterday, the day before or even this morning – if not two or three months ago – Kali Yuga did begin. Two or three months ago a practitioner of black magic from hell had come to where we cooks get together. He handed out this red powder but *only* to us cooks. We chewed it with beetle-nut leaf *(puts a pinch of the red powder into his mouth)*, and streams of spittle flew out of our mouths and splattered all over us! So immediately that reciter of black magic spells announced that Kali Yuga had begun. And then what? Well, Kali Yuga seemed to have begun! And ever since Kali Yuga started, we cooks just don't feel comfortable until we put this red powder into our mouths.

VIDYADHARA

What red powder! Show me! Stay there; stay there. Don't come close, or else Kali might enter into my body.

SIDDHAPAKA

You are a great one to talk to me about staying away from you! Isn't my spittle already showering all over your body?

VIDYADHARA

Why is it called red powder?

SIDDHAPAKA

That black magic fellow told us why. It is always in the mouths of the red people of hell – hence, it is called Red-Faced, that is, *Tamramukhi* or tobacco. Take, you take, a little …

VIDYADHARA

Ugh! I won't even touch it.

SIDDHAPAKA

Come on! When Kali Yuga is in full swing, even your Guruji will chew it while teaching you. Anyway, I was going to ask you how many more days will you continue to study these religious books? It is almost two or three months since the beginning of Kali Yuga. So now people will respect us cooks and bartenders more than they do scholars and educated people.

VIDYADHARA

No, nobody respects us. Guruji and several other leading pundits had gone to bless Kichaka Maharaja yesterday. They had to wait at his door for two hours. Then he sent them a message saying that the pundits in Dharmaraja's palace in Indraprastha had first stuffed themselves and then got the Pandavas sent into exile, but Kichaka is not one to get so trapped by pundits!

SIDDHAPAKA

You have studied lots and lots, but who bothers with that? After endless requests to Kichaka Maharaja, you might get a low-level job working under some Anu-Kichaka. So I tell you, throw away this religious book, and either take a cook's slotted spoon in hand or open a liquor shop.

VIDYADHARA

We are Brahmins by caste, and we won't be able to manage a liquor shop. I have heard that along with customers, an owner also has to drink some liquor!

SIDDHAPAKA

People say you pundits don't even have as much brains as we cooks do – looks like that's true. If you are a Brahmin, then sell only sealed bottles. If you open a liquor shop, you might get some appreciation from Kichaka or an Anu-Kichaka. If you can't do that, take this slotted spoon, and you will earn a bigger salary than a pundit employed by an Anu-Kichaka. Oh, my, it's got quite late! I'll go.

VIDYADHARA

One moment! You were going to be appointed as an assistant to Chef Ballabha – what happened to that?

SIDDHAPAKA

You are a great pundit, and you ask questions like a man fast asleep? The day Kichaka Maharaja arrived, that's the very day I was appointed!

VIDYADHARA

My Guruji doesn't have any influence with Kichaka or Anu-Kichakas. Please get me a job somewhere through Chef Ballabha.

SIDDHAPAKA

Come see me later – I'll think about it. But first throw away that sacred book.

(Leaves)

VIDYADHARA

What he is saying is not untrue. As goes the sovereign, so go his subjects. In Matsyadesha Virata Maharaja is a king who merely sits on the throne, but Kichaka and the Anu-Kichakas are the real rulers. So needy students like me must give up our education. Now I will return this sacred book to Guruji, and open a liquor shop, or take a cook's slotted spoon, or make supplications to Siddhapaka for a job. I think it's best to appeal to him alone.

(Leaves)

Scene 4

Place: Palace of Rani Ratnaprabha. Ratnaprabha is sitting on her bed.

RATNAPRABHA

Mandahasini, listen Mandahasini, come here.

(Mandahasini enters)

MANDAHASINI

What is your command, Rani Saheb?

RATNAPRABHA

You know I don't wear jewelry at this time; I don't even touch this garland of flowers at night. Why do I have to tell you this every day! Shouldn't a person be able to remember at least this much?

MANDAHASINI

Rani Saheb, from the day Maharaja returned from Hastinapura, I started keeping your jewels and garland of flowers at night here.

RATNAPRABHA

Unless it is certain that *swari* will be coming to my palace, don't keep these things by my bedside. Today it's six days since he arrived, but because he is so busy with matters of state that he hasn't had the time to say a single word to me. Why should I get all decked up? Take everything away. *(As Mandahasini takes away the box of jewelry and garland of flowers, Kichaka enters carrying another box and stands behind Ratnaprabha)* When the person for whom I should be adorning myself isn't around, why should I put on all these ornaments?

KICHAKA

Here I am near you, and the jewels have not gone far either.

RATNAPRABHA

When a woman's foremost jewel is near, what's the need for other jewels! It's been many days since you returned from Hastinapura, how did you remember this dasi today?

KICHAKA

How's it possible for me to not remember? A goddess whom I was thinking of constantly in Hastinapura, why would I even have to *remember* to gain her darshana?

RATNAPRABHA

Then it would seem that to take just four steps towards my palace you needed six to seven days?

KICHAKA

Well, that's true! To attain your darshana I had to move step by step, one day for each step, thinking about how to prepare suitably for the event! Which jewels would please Ratnaprabha, I had to assess that; that was step one; then I had to prepare the ornaments; that was step two; then came the third step; and so on! Just to make sure that you wouldn't be unhappy, many days went by in making these arrangements!

RATNAPRABHA

I was worried that while you were going on thinking like that, I might have to spend years or even my whole life waiting for you!

KICHAKA

My beloved, the real reason for my not coming to see you earlier is the command in the scriptures, "One should not greet the king or the Goddess with empty hands." And you know that I acknowledge only Emperor of India Duryodhana as my King and you as my chief goddess. I am not lying; don't think I am simply flattering you because I am in your presence.

RATNAPRABHA

Only naive women judge a man by his words; I have now learned to judge a man by his actions!

KICHAKA

Don't believe my words *(shows the jewels)*. Will you see my actions or not? This is not the box your servant took away from here. This is not the garland made by your dasi. Come, come close here, sit, and judge me by my actions. These are originally Draupadi's jewels, given to me in advance by the Kauravas, because ultimately she is going to be in my natakashala; these jewels … why did you turn your face away? Don't like them!

RATNAPRABHA

Like all women, I feel that the whole world's greatness should be bestowed upon you, but you think it is great to make other men's wives your dasis.

KICHAKA

Stupid, truly stupid! Ratnaprabha, you know that even if Draupadi or a beautiful angel from heaven comes to my natakashala, you alone will remain my true and supreme goddess.

RATNAPRABHA

Those are just words! Every day you admit a new dasi into your natakashala, but to see your supreme goddess you don't have the time for six or seven days!

KICHAKA

For six days I didn't come, that's true; but there was one good reason. These pearls and jewels of Draupadi were of the northern style, and to get them changed into our Matsyadesha style so that they adorn Ratnaprabha well, took me this long. I got delayed, punish me for the crime by allowing me to put the garland of flowers and jewels on you. *(Kneels in front of her)* Give this devotee the privilege to worship his supreme goddess with flowers and jewels.

RATNAPRABHA

(Stands up and moves a few steps away)

I don't want these jewels or anything else. I understand superficial talk very well. The other day in everyone's presence, when I was right in front of your eyes, you made such a big show for Sairandhri, and now you are praising me! If a stranger heard your speech just now, he would think that Lord Rama of Ayodhya must have learned his dedication to one wife from you.

KICHAKA

I knew you would get angry, so even though I was late I made sure that all arrangements for the jewels were taken care of. Look at this new jewel to be worn on one's feet. No woman in Matsyadesha has seen it before. During the Rajasuya yajna when Arjuna went to battle with foreign rulers, the King of the Yavanas gave him this jewel as a tribute. When Dharmaraja gave away all the pearls and jewels got from foreign lands to Brahmins, this one was so precious that Draupadi kept it back for herself. Look at it. *(Shows it to her)*

RATNAPRABHA

(Takes it in her hands)

Ugh! It looks like what natakashala women wear on their dancing feet – a bit like their ankle bells. Would respectable women wear an ornament like this?

KICHAKA

Oh, come on! All the royal women of the *Kalyavanas* wear this is on their feet. It was Draupadi's favorite jewel. The Kauravas call it tordya, and nowadays all the women of Hastinapura proudly wear it!

RATNAPRABHA

Wear this! If little girls wear this, it might look alright; but it just cannot look nice on grown women.

KICHAKA

Maybe you shouldn't wear it while going to the temple. But night time in the palace is a naughty time, isn't it?

RATNAPRABHA

No talk of naughtiness. I have one request. If you grant it, I will wear this ornament; if not, I don't want it!

KICHAKA

(To himself)

Put a jewel in a woman's hand, and her heart just melts!

RATNAPRABHA

You can't even grant me my one request! How much thinking does that need!

KICHAKA

Why one? I will listen to a hundred requests. But when?

RATNAPRABHA

When?

KICHAKA

I will put these tordya on your feet with my own hands, and then this devotee will sit and worship his jeweled supreme goddess.

RATNAPRABHA

Then you must grant my request.

KICHAKA

Agreed; *(puts the ornament on her feet)* now sit on the bed. *(Holds her hand and tries to move towards the bed)* So you wanted to saunter with these tordya and show yourself off to me; that's why you pretended to be angry and walked away and stood so far, isn't it? Step lightly, Rani Saheb. Arrogant in your beauty, each step you are taking seems intended to insult me, to crush my pride underfoot, step by each step.

RATNAPRABHA

Enough of teasing me!

(They sit on the bed)

KICHAKA

Should I put these diamond bangles around your wrists first, or shall I put these pearls around your neck, or should I put this nose ring on first?

RATNAPRABHA

You don't have to do this much work; what if I put on these ornaments myself?

KICHAKA

No! No! Even if the goddess is pleased and begins to talk, the devotee must continue his worship. If your soft hands have to do this work, what then is this devotee for?

RATNAPRABHA

Hope you remember your promise that you will grant my request?

KICHAKA

Yes I do. Just as the legs of an elephant get trapped in a thicket of thorny scrub, a woman gets trapped in the clusters and chains of pearls and jewels and forgets her rage. Just to prove me wrong, don't you get angry again. I will grant you your wish. Let me put your nose ring on *(puts it on)*. Just as a bull is not likely to run away from his feeding trough, a woman is not likely to go against the wishes of a husband who puts a nose ring on her.

RATNAPRABHA

I won't get trapped by such talk. You have to honor my request.

KICHAKA

Right now the chains of my jewels are around your feet; the new nose ring is firmly in your nose; and I bet that at this time Ratnaprabha will not utter a single word that I would dislike. So what am I afraid of! Your highness, if you so wish, do me the favor of pronouncing your command – your slave is ready to serve you.

RATNAPRABHA

My only request is, leave Sairandhri.

KICHAKA

Why? If I keep Sairandhri in my natakashala, what do you lose? There are so many other women in the natakashala; she will be just one of them.

RATNAPRABHA

No, I will not rest until I get a promise from you that you will leave Sairandhri. You have to make that promise.

KICHAKA

Ratnaprabha, you have known my nature over so many years; yet a beautiful angel like you could feel jealous of Sairandhri – that's a real surprise!

RATNAPRABHA

I am not asking you out of jealousy. If Sairandhri is unwilling to live in your natakashala, then is it manly for a valiant man like you to force her? She has been crying constantly now for four or five days. Maharaja, when a man oppresses a woman, he can never imagine how much grief he brings to the heart of a *pativrata*.

Kichaka-Vadha (The Slaying of Kichaka, 1907)

You have to be a woman to understand a woman's grief. Maharaja, you know with complete certainty how my heart is unwaveringly devoted to you. If I were in Sairandhri's situation today, think how my humiliation would have pained both you and me. My only request is that you consider how tormenting the wife of another man will stain the great name and reputation you have earned so far.

KICHAKA

Ratnaprabha, what you say is right; but you are forgetting one thing. We are the rulers, and Sairandhri is at our disposal. So the laws that apply to you do not apply to Sairandhri. Rulers are rulers, and servants are servants; we must always keep this distinction in mind.

RATNAPRABHA

But, Maharaja, how can you feel that any wife simply because she is not from among the rulers should be ready to sacrifice her modesty?

KICHAKA

Why shouldn't I feel that way? Otherwise, the natakashalas of Kichaka and Anu-Kichakas would not be so grand!

RATNAPRABHA

That may be so, but I don't like what you are doing at all. Since you always honor my word, I plead with you. Mighty Raja Ravana tried to subjugate Sita thinking she was the wife of a humble man wandering through the forest; keep in mind what happened then, and leave Sairandhri.

KICHAKA

Ratnaprabha, wasted, just wasted, all the years you spent with me have been wasted! I already told you earlier there's no need for you to feel jealous just because Sairandhri will be in my natakashala. No woman in the entire universe has the power to diminish my love for you. I saw Sairandhri is nice looking, so casually I asked for her! But now that I can see I am not getting her, no matter because of whom or what, Kichaka is not one to just shut up and sit down. If Sudeshana had sent Sairandhri to me immediately upon my asking, if Sairandhri had not had the guts to oppose me, then Ratnaprabha, I would have respected your words and not touched Sairandhri's body. And for your sake I would have sent her back to her husband's home with honor. But …

RATNAPRABHA

But what? What's humiliating about doing what you say you would have done? If you do it, your fame will spread far and wide, and holy men and saints will sing ballads about it in heaven.

KICHAKA

What a stupid thought! We rulers value our reputation here on earth far more than ballads in heaven. Our word should never be disobeyed. If dasis disobey me, people in the streets will start calling you that Coward Kichaka's wife. Shouldn't I think about that! Once a command has been issued, there is nothing further to think about it. If you think it an honor to be the wife of a man who takes back his orders from day to day, then Ratnaprabha is not fit to share the throne with me. This Sairandhri is merely the wife of a servant, but even if she were the wife of an expert chariot-borne warrior, or a famous chariot-borne warrior or even a legendary chariot-borne warrior, and not only that, but even if she were the wife of a prominent Anu-Kichaka himself, she would have to come to my natakashala by the time I announced. Turn away; go ahead, turn your face away. I will prove my word, even if I have to sacrifice Ratnaprabha's love!

(Curtain)

ACT THREE

Scene 1

Place: Courtyard of the Palace.
Enter: Maitreya, Saudamini, and Kichaka's two dasis, First Dasi and Second Dasi.

MAITREYA

Hello, girls, where are you going! If you have an escort, where is he? Or, are you just running around here and there in the courtyard with fans in your hands?

FIRST DASI

Kichaka Maharaja will soon be arriving here, so we have come.

SECOND DASI

Maharaja brought us here to see how *Brihannada* gives music lessons to the Rani Saheb.

MAITREYA

Can you sing anything?

SAUDAMINI

You need a good voice to sing. Is your voice good?

MAITREYA

Why do you need a good voice? Before Brihannada came here the Maharaja had put me in charge of giving music lessons. When I used to teach, I never insisted that the singer have a good voice. Once you sit down to sing, what difference does it make to music if your voice is not good, or even if you sing like a donkey?

FIRST DASI

Wish we had been here when Virata Maharaja had assigned you to teach the music class.

SECOND DASI

Even now if you could teach once in a while, we will surely come to learn.

MAITREYA

Even if your voice is cracked, it will be fine in my music. Only your feet have to be strong. Because my music should be performed with a constant tapping of the feet. I won't be able to teach my foot-tapping songs to a lame person.

FIRST DASI

Our feet are strong.

SECOND DASI

We can easily run one or two laps.

MAITREYA

Then show me how you will run to fast music.

(The dasis run and exit)

Saudamini, compared to you, the new dasis seem much smarter. I taught you for so long, but it was like pouring water into an overturned water pot!

SAUDAMINI

I am embarrassed to learn singing from a man, but now I can learn from the eunuch Brihannada. Of course, there's no problem in learning from an old man like you.

MAITREYA

It's good that this Brihannada has come; I was getting bored of this old age. Whenever anyone's daughter wants to learn music, then summon this old man – as if this old man is not a man!

SAUDAMINI

So Brihannada's arrival in our city has proven a great loss for our girls?

MAITREYA

And how is that?

SAUDAMINI

They have lost the opportunity of learning from an old and erudite guru like you!

MAITREYA

Why so much flattery today? Looks like you want me to do something?

SAUDAMINI

No, nothing! But there *is* a small thing. You are friends with Kankabhatta, and I suspect Sairandhri is close to Kankabhatta.

MAITREYA

Yes, Sairandhri is close to Kankabhatta, so what?

SAUDAMINI

The Rani Saheb has ordered me to make Sairandhri change her mind and go to Kichaka Maharaja's palace. So if you could talk to Kankabhatta about persuading Sairandhri.

MAITREYA

Kankabhatta is a poor Brahmin; he does have a gambling habit, but other than that – oh, great! Virata Maharaja and Maharani Saheb are coming right here.

(Virata and Sudeshana enter)

VIRATA

To a trivial matter Kichaka Maharaja gives such importance – I am amazed by it! If a dasi does not want to live in anyone's natakashala, she should be praised for it. Kichaka Maharaja is your brother, and besides that, Kichaka and the Anu-Kichakas are the main pillars of my kingdom; so Kichaka is dearer to me than my own life; I don't even need to say this. But what's the point of this much arrogance over such a minor matter?

SUDESHANA

How is this a minor matter? The period of four days specified by Kichaka Maharaja is over today; I am afraid about what is going to happen now. Wars are fought over women. During my swayamvara you defeated so many princes; do you remember?

VIRATA

There could be a war over a princess, I agree; but a war over a dasi? That's impossible – we rulers and kings have not yet become so stupid.

SUDESHANA

Had Kichaka been as calm as you – not so impulsive and hot tempered – then there wouldn't have been such a hue and cry over a minor matter. But you know how stubborn Kichaka Maharaja is.

VIRATA

Kichaka Maharaja is certainly stubborn; but tell me, Maitreya, why should Sairandhri be so stubborn?

MAITREYA

That's what I say, too. Since Kichaka Maharaja himself is so pleased, why should she be so stubborn? Anyway, if Sairandhri had been with Maharani Draupadi in Indraprastha, would she have made such a fuss?

VIRATA

What do you mean?

MAITREYA

If the employer herself has five husbands, then how could a dasi of Indraprastha insist on being pativrata to only one husband?

SUDESHANA

Oh Saudamini, have you explained everything to Sairandhri?

SAUDAMINI

Sairandhri has gone to Vasant Garden to pick flowers, and Kankabhattaji has gone there as well; so I was going there with Maitreya Bhattji to see Sairandhri; and just then your Highnesses arrived.

VIRATA

We are going towards Vasant Garden. Send Sairandhri to us, so that we can personally enquire about this whole thing and talk to her about what is best for her.

(Virata and Sudeshana leave)

MAITREYA

Actually, Saudamini, had you been in Sairandhri's place, today *you* would have been adored! Virata Maharaja would have made entreaties to you! Sudeshana Maharani Saheb would have gladly accepted a job as your servant!

SAUDAMINI

That's so true, Maitreya Bhattji. After all how are my looks any different from Sairandhri's? I am sure, if not today then tomorrow, Kichaka Maharaja's heart is bound to be attracted to me. Bhattji Maharaja, tell me honestly do I look any worse than Sairandhri?

MAITREYA

Turn your face towards me – let me study your looks. The hair is arrogantly thrusting itself to the front – it should be pushed back. The nose is odd and huge – it should be peeled and pared down. The eyes are tiny. The ample flesh around the hips should be shrunk, the pond of the eyes should be enlarged, the flat cheeks should be puffed up, and then you will look exactly like Sairandhri!

(Kichaka enters with his two dasis)

KICHAKA

Where is Sairandhri? Maitreya, where is Sairandhri?

MAITREYA

Tomorrow's Sairandhri is standing here; today's Sairandhri …

Kichaka-Vadha (The Slaying of Kichaka, 1907)

KICHAKA

Maitreya, whom to make fun of and when, haven't you realized that even at your ripe age?

MAITREYA

One loses one's edge in old age! Just as I make fun of this dasi, I tried to make fun of you – forgive me.

KICHAKA

Why girls, I told you to find Sairandhri, and you haven't been able to find out anything, right?

FIRST DASI

I looked for her in the dance school.

SECOND DASI

I searched for her in the art school.

FIRST DASI

I asked about her in the music school.

SECOND DASI

I enquired about her in the kitchen.

MAITREYA

She is nowhere in the palace! Did you look for her outside Brihannada's school? Your lordship, these girls won't be able to find Sairandhri. If the hunting dogs are here, could the hunters be far behind? So reason the rabbits and hide in fright.

KICHAKA

Maitreya, if you tell me exactly where Sairandhri is at this moment I will give you a big reward.

SAUDAMINI

Sairandhri is in Vasant Garden at this moment plucking flowers.

KICHAKA

Here take your reward. *(Gives her a pearl necklace)*

MAITREYA

In the vast Vasant forest, is Sairandhri in the western woods, or in the southern pond playing with the swans, or plucking lotus in the northern pond, or weaving a garland of flowers in the central hut? Even before she has spoken of any particular location, his lordship has given away the reward! I never realized his lordship had become so desperate for Sairandhri.

KICHAKA

Let's go to Vasant Garden. Now you must find the place precisely.

(Kichaka leaves with his two dasis)

MAITREYA

You told him Sairandhri's whereabouts, and you got this pearl necklace, Now if you can get Sairandhri to go to his natakashala, he will be so pleased with you that instead of keeping Sairandhri he will keep you.

SAUDAMINI

A second after the first, a third after the second, this is how men choose women.

(Ratnaprabha and Mandahasini enter)

MAITREYA

Ratnaprabha Rani Saheb has come; she must be searching for Kichaka Maharaja. I will tell her Maharaja's whereabouts and earn a reward. Don't you dare interfere; stand quietly as if your mouth is tied shut thus.

(Maitreya takes Saudamini's hand, places it over her mouth and makes her stand still)

RATNAPRABHA

I don't think Sairandhri can have such a firm resolve. If Maharaja entreats her nicely in private, it's impossible for her resolution to not waver. His eyes have some magical power, and they seem to shower you with shafts of irresistible enchantment!

MANDAHASINI

Bai Saheb, Sairandhri is really a rare kind of woman. Her conduct will put to shame even one who practices meditation; everyone here knows that.

RATNAPRABHA

That's all true, but didn't she come from the Kaurava durbar? That's what makes me afraid. The Kauravas' ancestors married Devayani, and Devayani's demon daughter Sharmishtha produced all their subsequent generations. As a descendant of that clan, Sairandhri must know instinctively how to wrest control of the master's heart and how to throw his wife out of the house.

MANDAHASINI

But Bai Saheb will have a different experience with Sairandhri.

RATNAPRABHA

Ever since Draupadi's swayamvara, Sairandhri had been in her service, and during that time the Pandavas never ignored Draupadi; so maybe someone like her does have a good character. Oh Saudamini, why are you standing there and grinning like that, with your mouth wide open and showing everyone your ugly teeth?

MANDAHASINI

Really, Bai Saheb, her mouth and teeth look frozen in place! Usually, her tongue is wagging constantly, carrying on without ever pausing!

MAITREYA

Don't you dare give the news first. Maharani Saheb, I must first understand what reward you plan to give me; otherwise, like her, I too will stand there with my mouth frozen in place!

RATNAPRABHA

But reward for what?

MAITREYA

For what! I won't accept a small reward. Because she told him the whereabouts of Sairandhri, Kichaka Maharaja gave her a pearl necklace. You should give me a bigger reward. Women, compared to men, are not misers; men have to labor to earn, but women get jewels and pearls for free. So unless I know beforehand exactly how many necklaces I will get, I won't say a single word about how Kichaka Maharaja is roaming in Vasant Garden looking for Sairandhri.

(Puts his hands on his mouth and remains frozen in place)

RATNAPRABHA

Mandahasini, take me to Vasant Garden. He might be harassing Sairandhri; I must reach there in time.

MANDAHASINI

Here, come from this side, Bai Saheb.

(Mandahasini and Ratnaprabha leave. Maitreya and Saudamini remain frozen with hands on their mouths but soon start making signs to each other)

MAITREYA

Until I get a reward, I am going to hold my mouth shut.

SAUDAMINI

Until you say it's okay to talk, I am going to hold my mouth shut.

MAITREYA

How long do we stand here like dumb people?

SAUDAMINI

Ratnaprabha Rani Saheb fooled you, what can I do?

MAITREYA

Women are shrewd; you got a necklace. We men are innocent!

SAUDAMINI

Men, and innocent, really?! They are too clever for their own good!

MAITREYA

Clever and thus with an empty bullock cart! From now on *you* have to show me a strategy or two for winning some rewards.

SAUDAMINI

Through Kankabhatta change Sairandhri's mind.

MAITREYA

OK, take your hand off your mouth. Let's go to Vasant Garden to find Kankabhatta. Show me the way to Vasant Garden.

SAUDAMINI

Come this way, Bhattji Maharaja.

MAITREYA

You guide me along, and shout out your instructions loudly.

SAUDAMINI

Step forward slowly, Bhattji Maharaja. You might stumble. Step forward slowly. There is a rock here. If you hit it, you will break your teeth.

MAITREYA

All my teeth have already fallen off. These are dentures. Guide me along, and speak loudly.

SAUDAMINI

Step softly; come this way, Maharaja. Step softly.

(They leave)

Scene 2

Place: Vasant Garden. Kankabhatta and Ballabha are sitting on a rock. Sairandhri is standing.

SAIRANDHRI

Maharaja, the constellation of stars at my birth was so strange that nothing in my life happens without complications. At the occasion of my swayamvara, father set up such a challenge that my dada was afraid that none of the Kshatriyas would win and Draupadi might remain unmarried. Then, mortified that Karna might win the challenge by aiming at the eye of that fish, I declared that I would never marry a person of low birth. At that time proud Karna did not even move from his seat. I was rescued from the persecution of that *sarathiputra* from our own country. But this lowly Kichaka – the Sarathiputra of Matsyadesha – is a threat that I just don't know how to escape. His saintly wife Ratnaprabha gave him a real earful; I called him a demon and a beast; Sudeshana Maharani Saheb tried to reason with him at great length, but nothing has worked. So now either he should be removed from this world, or I should disappear; otherwise, this problem will not go away.

KANKABHATTA

I don't like either of these solutions. Remove Kichaka from the world – that's easy to say, but undertaking it is far more difficult.

BALLABHA

How's that difficult? Dada, I await your command. Just as I destroyed Jarasandha, crushed the cannibal Bakasura and sent him to hell even as I ate the offerings sent to him, just as I made the Demon Kirmir of the Kamyaka Forest vanish within seconds, so will I – the moment you give the command – name the place, name the time and name the method – cut Kichaka's body into a thousand pieces and throw a piece in every Anu-Kichaka's house to make all the Anu-Kichakas shudder in fear of us.

SAIRANDHRI

Only such an action will stop an atrocity like this from happening again and again.

KANKABHATTA

What is achieved by piling one calamity onto another? Bhima, your might is enormous, and even if every Anu-Kichaka became arrogant like Kichaka you have the power to straighten them all out, but …

SAIRANDHRI

But what? By always behaving like this, you brought upon us all the forest exile and then this exile in disguise. Had you crushed the enemy then and there, would this despicable sarathiputra have ever set his eyes on me? Toward an avowed enemy, why behave with justice and compassion? Maharaja, if we are compassionate towards a viper and let it escape, then tomorrow won't the responsibility for the deaths of those killed by that viper not fall on our heads? To avoid the sin of future murders, be cruel and unkind today; this is the way of truth, I feel.

KANKABHATTA

That sometimes the goddess of justice has to pretend to be heartless is true, but, Draupadi, if the heartlessness is only for our own good, then the almighty will not rest until he brands it a sin, even if the action was based on calm and careful consideration. To be cruel today so as to gain happiness for oneself tomorrow is like getting trapped in a cycle of greed. If I bring grief to someone out of selfishness, then that person will actually reap great benefit from that grief; I believe the goddess of justice will always regard any deed of cruelty as a sin.

SAIRANDHRI

So then should one never punish one's enemies? Maharaja, how on earth were you born into the warrior Kshatriyas caste, I wonder again and again!

BALLABHA

When evil Duhshasana touched Draupadi's sari and my eyes became red with anger but your demeanor remained as calm as in deep meditation, that's the time I started to doubt if you and I could have been born of the same mother Kunti; and today that doubt has been doubled. Maharaja, if you don't want to fight with anyone in any manner and care only for the well-being of strangers, why did you accept this exile in disguise after we had completed our exile in the forest? Your vow to be Ajatashatru – the one without enemies – would have been fulfilled if we had simply remained in our forest exile for the rest of this life.

SAIRANDHRI

And those brothers of yours who gave up the comforts of the royal world for the sake of your devotion to truth, those brothers of yours at your insistence would have agreed to live in exile for the remainder of this life.

BALLABHA

Maharaja, a war cannot be fought without cruelty and heartlessness. When you release your bow the enemy should willingly and happily agree to die – will we human Kshatriyas ever secure such a skill of war?

SAIRANDHRI

Upon losing their men in war which enemies' wives will not weep? I think once we somehow complete these days of our exile in disguise, and then Duryodhana refuses to give you back your share of the kingdom, you will worry that a war against the Kauravas will turn their wives into widows and thus decide to take the road to another forest exile!

KANKABHATTA

Draupadi, Bhima, I am telling you again very clearly, put aside today's question about killing Kichaka, but tomorrow after our total exile is over, and unless I see the Kauravas' sins getting out of hand and unless I am convinced that apart from destroying them there is no other alternative, I will not give permission to kill Duryodhana – even on a battlefield.

SAIRANDHRI

Maharaja, I have done no harm to that evil man Kichaka's body, soul or mind. Despite that, his heart is filled with sinful designs on me, and even his sister Sudeshana and wife Ratnaprabha have given up on changing his mind; so it's time to kill Kichaka for committing such a grave sin and do both Kichaka and the Anu-Kichakas a favor – isn't the moment to save them from themselves here yet?

BALLABHA

The Pandavas have never desired even a tiny piece of a trifle belonging to Kichaka or the Anu-Kichakas. The Pandavas have never wished even for a second to put any obstacle in the proper happiness and peace of Kichaka or the Anu-Kichakas. Even though we have treated him in this manner, Kichaka wants to kidnap our source of happiness, our treasure – this noble and pious Draupadi – and rape her. Without fear of god or dharma, he arrogantly indulges in all sinful pleasures just as he wishes. Kichaka and the Anu-Kichakas are ready to force the blameless sadhu-like Pandavas into circumstances more painful than experienced in generations and generations. In this situation, Ajatshatru Dharmaraja, will you not give this Bhima your permission to kill Kichaka?

KANKABHATTA

It's not that I will never give my permission, but methods other than killing have not yet been exhausted. Though Kichaka is not paying any heed to Sudeshana and Ratnaprabha, Virata Maharaja has the strength, if he wishes to use it, to stop Kichaka from committing this sin.

(Offstage announcement: "Attention! Maharaja Adhiraja Virata Maharaja has arrived in Vasant Palace. All players of dice should assemble there. This is the order of the Maharaja.")

Draupadi, in this garden today a game of dice has been organized, and I have to be present there; I will bring the matter up with Maharaja, but until then don't get provoked into doing anything unwise.

(Leaves)

SAIRANDHRI

My beloved lord, your promise to kill one hundred Kauravas and braid my hair with hands stained with their blood seems unlikely to be fulfilled.

BALLABHA

Why, Draupadi, how can such needless doubts enter your mind? Unless the Kauravas die under the blows of my mace, this Bhima's birth will have been in vain.

SAIRANDHRI

During the Kaurava–Pandava battle you will show your valor as you promised, that I do not doubt. But since your elder brother is pursuing renown as a supposedly great lover of truth, none of you will have an opportunity to lift your weapons. My beloved lord, Kichaka will not hesitate to oppress me openly, and in this time of our disguise Draupadi …

BALLABHA

And all the Pandavas with Draupadi …

SAIRANDHRI

Will be finished.

BALLABHA

Don't have any such fear. If it comes to that I won't hesitate to drag Kichaka off his chariot on the public road as everyone looks on and kick him to death; that's my firm resolve.

SAIRANDHRI

But that will reveal the Pandavas' disguise and under the terms of our agreement we will have to spend another twelve years in exile; instead I should disappear …

BALLABHA

My pledge to braid your hair with hands stained in the blood of the Kauravas will never be broken. Draupadi, henceforth, I will not bother about Dharmaraja. Give me your command; I will kill Kichaka this very second.

Kichaka-Vadha (The Slaying of Kichaka, 1907)

(Offstage. Kichaka: "Girls, search for Sairandhri in all four corners of the flower garden, and I will go rest a bit in the mango orchard beyond.")

Sairandhri, look, Kichaka is coming right here. Now give me the order. I will at this very moment crush Kichaka and throw him into the trees! Oh! If I had Dharmaraja's permission, this was the best opportunity to kill Kichaka. Panchali, shall I hurl this bully to the underworld?

SAIRANDHRI

No, my beloved lord, no. Without Dharmaraja's permission we cannot kill Kichaka. We'll get some other opportunity later.

BALLABHA

Then you and I should not be seen together at one spot.

SAIRANDHRI

You go hide in those trees, and with you so near I won't be afraid at all. And if it comes to it, I will scream so loudly that my voice will reach Vasant Mahal.

(Ballabha goes and hides)

(To herself)

When I see this evil barbarian I think of Duhshasana. Unless I first see this reprobate's blood on Bhima's hands, I doubt if the Kauravas' blood will ever wet my hair. Until Dharmaraja hears this degenerate harassing me with sinful and offensive words, his anger's flame will not burn bright. To rouse men to perilous action, anger is indispensable.

(Kichaka enters)

KICHAKA

(To himself)

Good, I saw her. Now I will drag her to my palace. Where can she go? It was my mistake to spare her on the very first day. These dasas and dasis need to be kicked every now and then. I have ordered all my Anu-Kichakas never to talk nicely to our dasas and dasis, not even for a second. Kick them while getting up, shove them while sitting down; if we don't treat them like this, they think they are the equals of us Kichakas and Anu-Kichakas, they resent our grandeur, and they find our reign oppressive. We just have to do this. Actually, I should tie her by her limbs and drag her along the road to my palace. *(Sits down)* Sairandhri, come, come and stand close to me. What are you doing here?

SAIRANDHRI

I am plucking flowers for Sudeshana Maharani Saheb.

KICHAKA

Sairandhri, I like you, so I am honoring you by allowing you to live in my natakashala. I am doing this as a favor to you. You used to be Draupadi's dasi, right? Soon Draupadi will also be coming to my natakashala; but don't worry at all that you might have to serve as her dasi again. The rule in my natakashala is to never dig into the previous status of the women, never ask who had a high rank or who had a low rank; once they enter my natakashala, all the women have the same rank. You should not think that when Draupadi comes here she will remind you of your past lowly status and humiliate you. In my natakashala everyone is provided the same respect and the same rank. You should know, Sairandhri, that until today this Kichaka has never pleaded with anyone; but let me tell you something for your own good. If you come to my natakashala willingly and please me, then I will do you a favor; but you must show me by your conduct that you are ready to accept this favor. The favor I will bestow upon you is this: when I see Draupadi

Kichaka-Vadha (The Slaying of Kichaka, 1907)

here I will make her your dasi! Think carefully about this trust that I have in you, and behave accordingly; otherwise, the sympathy I have for you ...

SAIRANDHRI

Filthy Sutaputra, watch your tongue. Though you see this Sairandhri in the garb of your dasi today, the might of all divine Yakshas is set to protect me, as you will realize.

KICHAKA

Sairandhri, with these words you are destroying the empathy my heart feels for you. To such empty words and threats, resolute and strong men like me never pay any heed. Your exertions to alarm me are futile. For this you will definitely pay a heavy price. You are the daughter of a lowly man, the wife of a servant; why do you want to look ridiculous by telling stories about the might of Yakshas? You've probably spent your nights with someone who cannot even dream about wealth. You've probably spent your days in a beggar's shack, wearing rags and eating from earthen pots, but, dear Sairandhri, you should praise the almighty for making your body so beautiful that, even though you are without any social standing or able forbears, a powerful and aristocratic man like me does not mind spending time with you in seclusion. Sairandhri, put on these garments and jewels that even heavenly nymphs find rare and precious, and agree to live in my pleasure palace, to the envy of the Queen of Heaven Indrani herself, and, Sairandhri, with your passion wrest total control of the heart of this man Kichaka, at whose feet all the world's rulers wait, and become his natakashala's incomparable jewel.

SAIRANDHRI

You wicked man, only because of the help from the Anu-Kichakas you can treat Virata Maharaja with disdain and strut around bragging that no man in Matsyadesha can surpass your power; but there is a god who will secure justice for everyone; keep this in mind. For trying to violate a pious woman, your power will be paralyzed, and your authority will collapse in no time. You sinner, angels with divine powers have been angered by your needlessly oppressing good people and are simply waiting for you to cross the line so that they can destroy you. You cannot see them because your eyes have been blinded by sins; but, you evil monster, keep this in mind, one more step on the path of evil, and these heavenly angels will appear here immediately. Those people who today are amazed at how in less than the time it takes to snap two fingers, you grabbed control of such an enormous kingdom and sidelined Virata, those same people will wonder how suddenly a sin or two destroyed Kichaka.

KICHAKA

Sairandhri, by telling me such well known stories, you are destroying yourself. You must come to my natakashala. This has been decided definitely and will not change. But with such unnecessary talk about good and evil, the sympathy I have for you …

SAIRANDHRI

Swine, what sympathy? Let your sympathy go to hell! With this talk of sympathy, sympathy, all you want is to make us all your whores! Someone like you should be ashamed even to talk about sympathy!

KICHAKA

(Stands) A whore is a whore, and yet she puts on the airs of a pativrata! Sairandhri, don't you have the brains to understand that if you were such a virtuous lady, why would you be serving as a dasi? Babble about just and unjust, and that too from a dasi! Sairandhri, what can you be thinking? The Kauravas tried to disrobe your mistress – Draupadi – in front of the mighty warriors and the great and elderly nobles of their court, but – I – this Kichaka – will have you stripped naked by some Anu-Kichaka's servant in the middle of the bazaar, and you will lose the honor

of joining my natakashala, and, not only that, you will have to spend your days as some petty Anu-Kichaka's kept whore. Come, let me take you to my palace. *(Holds her hand)* Summon your yakshas, kinnaras, angels; summon whoever was going to come to save you. In front of their eyes I will violate your modesty …

SAIRANDHRI

Help! Help! Protect this poor creature from that wicked beast.

KICHAKA

Come, angels of god or the great god Mahadeva, come; come whoever was going to come. Whoever has resolved to release Sairandhri from my grasp, come and show me. Come, come. *(Sairandhri screams towards Bhima's offstage hiding place)*. I invite everyone. All heavenly powers, visible or invisible, come. I will stop them all with just my left hand, and with my right hand I will pull your clothes off; if I don't take your modesty, this Kichaka will not spend a moment more on this earth. *(Sairandhri again screams towards the offstage Bhima. Kichaka pulls her sari pallava)* Summon anyone you want; scream again at the top of your lungs; show me which bull wants to come here to get slaughtered.

(Ratnaprabha and Sudeshana enter)

RATNAPRABHA AND SUDESHANA

(Together) Maharaja, what awful behavior, what a sin!

RATNAPRABHA

Leave her; leave the poor thing.

SUDESHANA

What is so manly in raping a poor helpless woman?

(Kichaka leaves Sairandhri)

KICHAKA

Sairandhri, no matter which man or how many multitudes of soldiers had come to your rescue, I would not have let you go today. But some incidents are so mysterious that a man has to surrender in front of the woman he is married to. It's true I am letting you go now, but the sun god in whose presence I was going to drag you away, that sun god will see you enter my natakashala before he sets. And when the sun opens his eyes again, he will see a Sairandhri who has been enjoyed by Kichaka. Sudeshana Maharani Saheb, this is my resolution. I have made it in the presence of the sun god and the anointed Maharani of Matsyadesha, and with my might I will make it a reality. If you wish that there not be any open enmity between Virata Maharaja and Kichaka and his Anu-Kichakas, then you will send this dasi to my pleasure palace tonight – adorned with jewelry, decked with garlands and bearing golden pitchers of intoxicating drinks. If she does not leave your palace before sunset, then I am nothing to Virata Maharaja, and Virata is nothing to me.

(Curtain)

ACT FOUR

Scene 1

Place: Courtyard of the royal palace. Enter Saudamini and Maitreya.

MAITRYEA

Changing Sairandhri's mind is beyond our ability.

SAUDAMINI

What does Kankabhatta say?

MAITREYA

Such gambling addicts! Virata Maharaja and Kankabhatta are totally lost in their game! Kankabhatta has no time to talk to me; and when Sudeshana Maharani Saheb and Ratnaprabha Rani Saheb came to see Maharaja, he had no time to talk to them. Just as gambling destroyed Yudhisthira Raja of the Pandavas, so will it destroy this Virata Raja. With all his gambling how can any time be left for governing? That's why Kichaka and Anu-Kichakas have become so powerful.

SAUDAMINI

Now is the time for action, but this Kankabhatta is lost in gambling! Awful addict! Just now Sudeshana Maharani Saheb has strictly ordered Sairandhri to go to Kichaka Maharaja's pleasure palace with golden decanters of liquor.

MAITREYA

So what did Sairandhri say?

SAUDAMINI

"I will kill myself but not let Kichaka touch my body."

MAITREYA

If she kills herself, you will benefit. One less competitor for you. Kichaka Maharaja will mourn for two days and then start chasing you.

SAUDAMINI

I have just come up with a trick! Let's do this. Persuade Sairandhri to merely step out of the palace into this courtyard with those golden decanters of liquor. And later, instead of her, I will carry those liquor decanters and enter Kichaka Maharaja's pleasure palace. Kichaka Maharaja always drinks in the evenings, but once he tastes liquor from my hands who knows what might or might not happen.

MAITREYA

That's a tremendous strategy! Tonight you will become a member of Kichaka Maharaja's natakashala. Then how many necklaces will you reward me with?

SAUDAMINI

You will get ample rewards, but do exactly as I say. Get Kankabhatta to coax Sairandhri to agree to our plan.

MAITREYA

That's my job; here I go.

(Leaves)

SAUDAMINI

(To herself)

Will this gamester Kankabhatta leave his game of dice and attend to such a matter? Don't depend on him. I must start this business through Chef Ballabha. Who's this coming here with a spoon in hand? Looks like Chef Ballabha's newly appointed assistant, Siddhapaka. If I talk to him, I can find out where Chef Ballabha is now.

(Siddhapaka and Vidyadhara enter)

Kichaka-Vadha (The Slaying of Kichaka, 1907)

SIDDHAPAKA

Vidyadhara, this is the very Dasi Saheb that Ballabha Maharaja sent us to see. Your stars must be in perfect alignment today; otherwise, we would not have been blessed with her darshana so soon! Fall; fall at her feet; right away, fall at her feet.

(Vidyadhara prostrates himself to offer greetings and then kneels and stays put with folded hands)

SAUDAMINI

Why Siddhapaka, what's all this drama?

SIDDHAPAKA

Great Dasi Saheb, he is a great pundit. He studied at Guruji's house for years … how many years, Vidyadhara?

VIDYADHARA

Twelve to fifteen years, Kindhearted Dasi Saheb.

SIDDHAPAKA

He studied for fifteen years with renowned and erudite scholars who have given him these recommendations. What's written in those papers? Tell her, tell her!

VIDYADHARA

That I won three competitions, Great Dasi Saheb.

SIDDHAPAKA

He is a great pundit. In pundit gatherings he shines like … like whom … let me think … like whom …? Names of old sages simply don't stay in my head. Like whom?

VIDYADHARA

Like Brihaspati, Compassionate Dasi Saheb.

SAUDAMINI

That's nice. So what …?

SIDDHAPAKA

So what happened is … what happened is … what happened, Vidyadhara?

VIDYADHARA

Didn't get a job anywhere, and so, Compassionate Great Dasi Saheb, I have been starving.

SAUDAMINI

I feel terrible at the plight of this pundit! Had the poor thing been born a woman rather than a man, I would have got him hired in some Anu-Kichaka's natakashala.

SIDDHAPAKA

He knows economics; he knows astrology; you know business, right?

VIDYADHARA

Yes, my lord.

SIDDHAPAKA

He knows mathematics … isn't it?

VIDYADHARA

Yes, Kind Master.

SIDDHAPAKA

You know history, don't you?

VIDYADHARA

Yes, My Lord.

SIDDHAPAKA

He knows essay writing. Don't you?

VIDYADHARA

Yes, Merciful Great Dasi Saheb.

SAUDAMINI

Get up; get up; tell me what you *don't* know; that will be shorter.

VIDYADHARA

(Gets up)

I don't know how to cook or how to get ingredients needed for cooking. I know everything else, Respected Ocean-of-Kindness Great Dasi Saheb.

SIDDHAPAKA

That's why he is dying of hunger, Great Dasi Saheb. It's true that he is a great pundit, but he can't fill his stomach by working as a dasi in some Anu-Kichaka's natakashala because he is not a woman. You are not a woman, right?

VIDYADHARA

Unfortunately, I was born a man, Fortunate Great Dasi Saheb.

SIDDHAPAKA

He could do business, but he has no capital. Do you have any?

VIDYADHARA

I spent everything on books, Twice-Blessed Great Dasi Saheb.

SIDDHAPAKA

Since he is starving like this, I will put in a good word for him with Chef Ballabha Maharaja. Why Chef Ballabha Maharaja? Because Kichaka Maharaja's heart is set on Sairandhri Dasi Saheb, and Sairandhri Dasi Saheb seems to favor Chef Ballabha Maharaja. So I wanted to use some influence through Sairandhri Dasi Saheb.

SAUDAMINI

Then does it mean you couldn't use any influence through Sairandhri?

SIDDHAPAKA

Ballabha Maharaja said that Sairandhri Dasi Saheb is upset these days, but from among the other Dasi Sahebs, no one has more influence with Kichaka Maharaja than you do, Saudamini Dasi Saheb. Kichaka Maharaja sometimes shows his affection for her by abusing her shamelessly or by calling her filthy names, said Ballabha Maharaja in praise of you. Ballabha Maharaja loves this poor pundit because of me, and now Ballabha Maharaja will himself come to intercede with you.

SAUDAMINI

Alright, when he comes, send him to that temple of goddess Mahalaxmi over there. *(To herself)* This Ballabha – for the sake of this pundit – is coming to plead for my influence; this is a great opportunity. Now through him I'll get Sairandhri to change her mind, and then this evening instead of Sairandhri, I will take the golden decanters of liquor and enter Kichaka Maharaja's pleasure palace.

(Leaves)

SIDDHAPAKA

Let's go, Vidyadhara, to Ballabha Maharaja. I am sure your mission has been successful. Nowadays there are two ways to bribe without money. One is to plead with a Kichaka or Anu-Kichaka's household cook. And the second is to fall at the feet of a Kichaka or Anu-Kichaka's dasi who is either secretly or openly a mistress in his natakashala!

VIDYADHARA

Now I have got double the influence. So I should get at least a low-level job.

Scene 2

Place: Front courtyard of Kichaka's pleasure palace.
Enter: Saudamini, with golden decanters of liquor in her hands; Sairandhri; and Ballabha.

SAUDAMINI

Sairandhri, I have never experienced the kind of happiness I am feeling today. I am sunk so deep into the tender and delightful thoughts of the approaching dark night that the red glow of the setting sun appears to bathe me in passionate moonlight, and you look like an angel who has come to chaperone me – a lady eager to be one with her lover – right to the doorstep of her lover's pleasure palace. Really, Sairandhri, every palace door I see on this road looks just like the door of his pleasure palace. No matter which man I see, I feel as if my lover has come. Twice or thrice when my eyes fell on this Ballabha walking with us, I thought Kichaka Maharaja had come and I felt so bashful!

BALLABHA

Actually, Saudamini, we have already arrived at Kichaka Maharaja's palace.
So take these liquor decanters from Sairandhri and go in and tell him that in
place of Sairandhri you have brought him the drinks.

(Sairandhri gives the liquor decanters to Saudamini)

SAUDAMINI

Sairandhri, now as we had planned, go to Virata Maharaja's durbar and plead with him. Here I will try to make Kichaka Maharaja happy, and if the almighty gives me success, then you too will have gained your wish. I have full confidence in my beauty – after tonight Kichaka Maharaja will definitely have no desire to bother you. Without any fear, go with Ballabha to Virata Maharaja's durbar. Now I will enter Kichaka Maharaja's palace.

(Saudamini leaves)

BALLABHA

Draupadi, we have somehow managed this time. Had Sudeshana Maharani not ordered you to leave immediately with the liquor decanters, we wouldn't have had a reason to consider the plan of this lowly dasi. But Virata Maharaja has told Dada that he will consider your appeal in the durbar this evening; and so far that's Maharani's command as well!

SAIRANDHRI

Seeing me leave with the decanters of liquor, Sudeshana Maharani Saheb was certainly relieved, but if she now finds me in the durbar she will again get angry.

BALLABHA

But Dada believes that Virata Maharaja will judge the appeal from your point of view, and so this whole problem will be easily resolved.

SAIRANDHRI

If that's his command, then I will go and make my appeal! When Virata Maharaja, Sudeshana Maharani Saheb and Ratnaprabha Rani Saheb all meet together in one place and hear me out, they will be inclined to render proper justice; I have no doubt about that. But, Maharaja, my heart fears that this villain Kichaka will grab me in the street or block my path into the durbar by standing in front of me like a demon. Kichaka and the Anu-Kichakas are so powerful today that even though Virata Maharaja clearly sees their injustice and atrocities, he has to stay silent in the face of their unyielding audacity. Kichaka's flagrant sinfulness, Maharaja, makes me feel as if atheism has taken over the world, and I think his evil conduct that insults even the almighty himself has driven all sages and saints to run and hide in forests and mountains. Maharaja, in my heart I am convinced that my appeal today will be of no use. That painful thorn jammed in our feet, rather than waiting for someone else to remove it, we should ourselves …

BALLABHA

Even if it does not gain us anything, it will at least satisfy Dada.

SAIRANDHRI

That is why I too am going to make the appeal. If a nasty and ill-behaved boy somehow gets hold of a sword and starts slashing away right and left, isn't it a man's duty to take that sword out of his hands for his welfare? This Kichaka persecutes poor defenseless people, and no matter how many times thoughtful men try to reason with him, he persists in this tyranny. Should we not remove from his hands the instrument of his tyranny – his depraved body? Is this not the sacred duty of everyone devoted to dharma?

BALLABHA

That's why I have been saying we must go to the durbar and make our appeal; that way Dharmaraja will grasp the whole situation, and we will get his permission to kill Kichaka. In any case, these durbar deliberations will take up the rest of the evening, and then nature's cycle will inevitably bring us the night for our action. Let's go, Sairandhri; walk fast or else, as you said, that fiend might catch us on the road itself, and then these hands might do something that will reveal our identities and thus force us into yet another twelve years of forest exile.

(Ballabha and Sairandhri leave)

(Kichaka and Saudamini enter from the opposite side of the stage; Kichaka is trying to drive Saudamini away)

KICHAKA

Scoundrel! Strumpet! Treacherous bitch! I will kick and break your back.

SAUDAMINI

I came here because of my blind love for you.

KICHAKA

I will poke both your eyes out and really blind you! And then I will throw you out. One kind word to such low-class people, and they presume straightaway that they are our equals. Shameless swine! Bazaar strumpet! Two-faced liar! Get out of here! So Sudeshana sent you here with the decanters of liquor! Just any whore from the bazaar will content Kichaka, is that how naïve you think I am? Looks like Virata and Sudeshana are proudly presuming that they can manage without me. Rogue, villain; *(kicks her)* first I will break your limbs and then your mistress' limbs.

SAUDAMINI

No, Sudeshana Bai Saheb did not send me here; Sairandhri and I came here together …

KICHAKA

Then where has Sairandhri gone?

SAUDAMINI

Sairandhri was heaping curses on you. Such a woman in your natakashala won't bring you any happiness. It was this thought and my love for you that spurred me into your palace; and Sairandhri went to the durbar.

KICHAKA

Is that so? Then for your treachery and duplicity I will drag you by your ears and look for Sairandhri. Wherever Sairandhri is, there I will drag you. Tonight I will fulfill my pledge. Virata, Sudeshana, or whoever tries to stop me from my pledge, I will crush them all under my feet. My action will make known to all Matsyadesha tonight that even god Brahma does not have the courage to contradict Kichaka's word and resolve.

(Leaves, dragging Saudamini by her ears)

Scene 3

Place: Virata's Durbar. Virata is seated on his throne. Sudeshana and Ratnaprabha are seated on one side, and Guru and Purohit on the other side. Dasas and dasis are fanning those present. Mandahasini is standing behind Ratnaprabha and Sudeshana and fanning them. Kankabhatta is standing behind Guru and Purohit.

VIRATA

Guru Maharaja, Purohit Maharaja, you have now heard the appeal made by Kankabhattaji. It is my desire to know from you what course dharma demands in this matter.

GURU

Maharaja, from the standpoint of dharma there is no room for any doubts on this subject. Dharma will never sanction one man's oppression of another.

PUROHIT

In some instances, dharma says that any man who rapes a woman must be given a life sentence; however, in some unavoidable circumstances …

GURU

To ensure conditions where the question of rape and its punishment does not even arise is the king's true duty. If such conditions prevail, then the issue of unavoidable circumstances is not relevant.

SUDESHANA

What's the use of discussing this? Sairandhri has already gone with decanters of liquor to Kichaka Maharaja. Because of Sairandhri's sensible willingness, there is no need for us to talk about any dangers.

KANKABHATTA

Maharani Saheb, it was only in order not to anger you that Sairandhri went to Kichaka Maharaja's palace with the liquor decanters. She knows that I have made this petition to the throne and that Maharaja has assured me of its consideration, so she will actually be giving those decanters to somebody else and will come here to the durbar soon.

RATNAPRABHA

Maharani Saheb, I kept feeling that Sairandhri was never going to agree to it of her own free will. No matter what others think, her talk of having help from yakshas and kinnaras might well be true. With that fear in my heart, I keep worrying about how to turn him away from his sinful intentions. If His Majesty would hear his sister's request and do her the great favor of going to his palace and explaining everything to him, then he will most surely honor His Majesty's words.

VIRATA

I just can't understand what to do in this situation. My mind feels warped: I find both good evil equally terrible. Kankabhattaji, there is a story about events from ten to twelve years ago; you used to be in the Kaurava–Pandava durbar, so you should know the story I am about to tell you. When the Pandavas left for exile, Maharishi Vyasa went to Dhritarashtra Maharaja's durbar and protested in every way he could about the evil deeds of Duryodhana, that is, Emperor Suyodhana. He firmly told Dhritarashtra Maharaja that in order to atone for the sin of sending the Pandavas into exile, he must desert Duryodhana. Dhritarashtra Maharaja's response at that time is worth remembering. Guru Maharaja, you are the one who told me this story five years ago, when you heard it in Hastinapura on your way back from your pilgrimage to the Himalayas.

GURU

Yes, Maharaja, I had almost forgotten it. Your Majesty's memory is astonishing!

PUROHIT

That goes without saying! Your Majesty, what did Dhritarashtra Maharaja answer?

VIRATA

Dhritarashtra Maharaja's response to the gathered sages was: "Even if Suyodhana becomes Duryodhana, he will still be my son. May his conduct always be good, and may his devotion to the path of truth lead him to heaven – that is my wish for him from the bottom of my heart, and that is what I will preach to him from time to time. I believe Suyodhana is now following the path of sin and pays no heed to what I taught him. You might say that it's out of my love for my son, or that I am very selfish like others, but I am not ready to push him away with my own hands. Perhaps with guidance from wise men like you, he will return to the path of truth; or perhaps if he gets hurt badly enough by his sinful ways, he will turn around and listen to my advice; with this hope I always keep Suyodhana close to my heart.

SUDESHANA

What did those sages say?

VIRATA

The sages began to curse Dhritarashtra, "Raja, understand that the time for the destruction of your entire family is coming near." But that wise Dhritarashtra reminded the sages of how he had discouraged Duryodhana and offered Draupadi a boon after the attempt to disrobe her in the Kaurava court. Then he begged all the sages to help change Duryodhana's heart and transform him back into Suyodhana.

RATANAPRABHA

What was the result of that request?

VIRATA

Since you already know how Duryodhana, the chief of the Kauravas, honored Kichaka Maharaja with the title of "Draupadi's Husband" in Hastinapura, there is no need for me to tell you that the sages' advice had no effect on his heart. Guru Maharaja, today I am feeling exactly as Dhritarashtra felt that day. Kichaka Maharaja is more dear to me than a brother, but his rape of Sairandhri is absolutely a sin; so I am in a real quandary about what I should do or not do. I just cannot come to a firm decision one way or the other. I know how tough it is to escape the grip of love and selfishness, so when I heard that Sairandhri had gone to Kichaka Maharaja's palace of her own accord, I thought that the calamity has passed.

KANKABHATTA

Maharaja, please forgive me for speaking out of turn. When a crime is being planned, a king must find and stop it at once – that's why royal thrones were established. Maharaja knows that during *Ramarajya*, the golden age of Rama's reign, sages held Rama responsible for even an ordinary man's untimely death. When orphan girls are raped at whim, and an oppressed populace endures its days in meek silence, and yet the ruler does not wake up and discharge his duty, then the foundation of dharma that undergirds a ruler's throne will weaken, and before long his kingdom will be destroyed. So it is my request to Your Majesty to forbid anyone from forcing this dasi to break her vow of pativrata; this is Your Majesty's sacred duty. No matter how much tyranny people put up with, in the durbar of god, no oppressive ruler will escape just retribution.

VIRATA

Kankabhattaji, I understand, but it's not so practical in the real world. Humans are born with a sense of dharma as much as a sense of self-interest: though I am a king,

I am also human. So if Sairandhri quietly sacrifices herself and gives in to the rape, I will turn a blind eye to Kichaka's action. But this afternoon in our Vasant Garden, the way Kichaka Maharaja grabbed Sairandhri's sari …

(Offstage. Sairandhri: "Scoundrel, demon, don't you dare touch my pallava … In Virata Maharaja's durbar who will I find to save my honor?")

VIRATA

Whose voice is this?

(Kichaka and Sairandhri enter; Kichaka is tugging at her sari pallava)

SAIRANDHRI

Avatar of dharma Virata Maharaja, protect this poor woman's modesty from this evil beast.

KICHAKA

Show me who will save this dasi.

Kichaka-Vadha (The Slaying of Kichaka, 1907)

VIRATA

In my durbar … in my presence … such behavior … I cannot tolerate.

GURU and PUROHIT *(together)*

What monstrous behavior!

SUDESHANA, RATNAPRABHA *(together)*

Behaving like a monster!

KICHAKA

(Kichaka continues to tug at Sairandhri's sari as she struggles to free herself)

Call my action monstrous or beastly, or consider it, Raja Virata, as my insult to you in your own presence. But this Kichaka – in this durbar, before the eyes of Raja, Rani, Guru, Purohit and all the others – before sunset – before the god of day who guides nature's cycle casts his last glance towards the earth – just as the god of night steals his first glimpse of the earth – in full view of them – this Kichaka – in this durbar – will tear the clothes off Sairandhri's body and make her realize that from tonight she will be my concubine.

SAIRANDHRI

Wicked man, demon, it looks like it's time for you to experience what power a pativrata possesses.

KICHAKA

Draupadi had five husbands, and you are her dasi! How does this bazaar whore Sairandhri have the pride of pativrata!

SAIRANDHRI

Virata Maharaja, you must protect this woman from this demon, or else …

KICHAKA

What, or else what? Maharaja, don't concern yourself. I want to see the miracle of her pativrata. Or else what? Speak.

KANKABHATTA

Kichaka Maharaja, remember the examples of pativratas like Sita, Mandodari, Savitri …

KICHAKA

Go to hell! I know the names of countless pativratas. Sudeshana, Ratnaprabha, Mandodari, Savitri and Sita are real pativratas, and our whore here calls herself a pativrata! This Kichaka is not one to pay heed to such threats. Sairandhri, think of all the pativratas from the beginning of time, and call on them for help; call on all future pativratas as well. This Kichaka has the power to crush under his feet the virtue of all pativratas, past and future, by defiling you … like this … by grabbing your pallava like this …

(All the men exclaim, "What's this? What's this?" as they gather around Kichaka. All the women begin crying as they plead, "We beg of you to leave her." Sairandhri keeps shouting, "Yakshas and kinnaras, the guardians of Sairandhri's honor, save me from this demon!")

KICHAKA

Let them come. The ones who call themselves yakshas and kinnaras or any other of your friends who want to rescue you, let them come. If any of your friends' desire for seeing you stark naked by daylight has not been fulfilled yet, Kichaka's hands will not rest until they have satisfied those eyes.

SAIRANDHRI

(Pushes away Kichaka's hand)

Virata Maharaja, if your hands do not stop this demon right away, my guardian yakshas will appear here, and your ancient throne will be covered in Kichaka's blood.

KANKABHATTA

Raja, if you don't want to destroy everyone, restrain this Kichaka. Abandoning dharma will ultimately destroy everyone.

(Repeat all, as above: All the men exclaim, "What's this? What's this?" as they gather around Kichaka. All the women begin crying as they plead, "We beg of you to leave her." Sairandhri keeps shouting, "Yakshas and kinnaras, the guardians of Sairandhri's honor, save me from this demon!")

KICHAKA

Come, Sairandhri's guardian yakshas and kinnaras; whoever wants to help, come quickly.

RATNAPRABHA

(Falls on her knees and holds Kichaka's feet)

Maharaja, such an inhuman act will cause the annihilation of our family line. Look at your wedded wife and don't do this. Maharaja, although you have no respect for past pativratas, nor any goodwill for future pativratas, you don't have any doubts about this poor dasi Ratnaprabha's love for you; at least, you can't feel any hatred for me. Maharaja, please remember the good times we shared together; recall how this poor dasi took care of you like a servant. And for the sake of my pativrata, promise this other half of yours not to dishonor any man's wife like this …

KICHAKA

Go, Sairandhri, go. At the moment I have released you. Get up, Ratnaprabha, get up; your jealousy has won the game this time. So, get up; get up.

RATNAPRABHA

No, Maharaja, no. Unless you promise me you will never again harass Sairandhri, I will not get up.

KICHAKA

Ratnaprabha, I have told you so many times, this should not be a cause for jealousy. This is a question of my reputation. To protect my reputation, to prove my word, I will do whatever I have to do. Get up; get up quietly. Tonight this Sairandhri must come to my natakashala.

RATNAPRABHA

Maharaja, stop this stubbornness.

KICHAKA

Get up; get up quietly. No…? No…? No…? Sairandhri, the pativratas of the past won't protect you; the pativratas of the future won't protect you; and the pativratas of the present won't protect you. This Kichaka has the power to tear apart the shackle of marriage clamped to his leg – with a kick like this and drag away Sairandhri.

(He kicks Ratnaprabha and goes to grab Sairandhri. The men rush forward with cries of "What recklessness!" "What recklessness!" Sudeshana shields Ratnaprabha, as both plead, "Maharaja, don't commit this sin")

SAIRANDHRI

(Stands behind the throne)

Virata Maharaja, I have come to your throne for sanctuary. To protect the honor of your throne, you have to guard my honor. You have the power to defend both.

KICHAKA

Raja Virata, I have only one thing to say to you. If you want me, then you must give Sairandhri to me right now. If you don't put Sairandhri under my control this very second, I will assume you don't want me, and so I will gather all the Anu-Kichakas and spend half the night, Raja Virata, destroying your throne, and the other half destroying this Sairandhri's pativrata. Raja Virata, you know well that this throne of yours that my might keeps steady, I can overthrow in less than a second. Raja, I am impatient for your answer.

SAIRANDHRI

Maharaja, before you answer, think carefully about what you decide. If you hand me over to this tyrant, along with his body this throne will also be torn into pieces – keep this clearly in mind. My sentinel yakshas and kinnaras will not only destroy Kichaka and the Anu-Kichakas but also all those who give consent to this evil act.

VIRATA

Guru Maharaja, Purohit Maharaja, at this critical juncture I will follow the example of Maharaja Dhritarashtra.

GURU and PUROHIT

At this time that course is most appropriate.

VIRATA

Kichaka Maharaja, before the Pandavas' exile when the Kauravas tried to disrobe Draupadi, the order that Dhritarashtra gave is the one I will give today, and you all must obey it.

KICHAKA

Raja, if your order is appropriate, I will certainly obey it.

VIRATA

Just as Dhritarashtra forbade Suyodhana from disrobing Draupadi in the packed Kaurava durbar, I forbid you from disrobing Sairandhri in my durbar. Just as Suyodhana was loved by Dhritarashtra, you are greatly loved by me, and I do not want to see you committing a sin before my eyes. At the same time I do not want you to wage war against me over a dasi, and so with immediate effect I will send this Sairandhri into exile in the forest. My envoy will now convey her to the temple of god Bhairava in the woods. Sairandhri, I have saved your honor in this durbar. But it is not politically prudent for me to make Kichaka Maharaja an enemy over a dasi like you; so in your forest exile do not depend on me but instead call your guardian yakshas and kinnaras for help.

(Curtain)

ACT FIVE

Scene 1

Place: Forest. Enter: Kankabhatta and Ballabha.

KANKABHATTA

Bhima, as we have no other choice I am giving you permission to slay Kichaka, but …

BALLABHA

But what?! Dada, I think even after I kill Kichaka you will have your "buts." Dada, I am so happy to get this opportunity to kill Kichaka in secret, and you are agitated and sad!

KANKABHATTA

That is true. What will happen? How will it happen? Are we committing any sins? Are we moving away from the righteous path shown by wise sages? When such thoughts arise, my heart becomes increasingly sad, and I feel exhausted by the world's affairs and wonder why Suyodhana's wager had not been one that required us to remain in forest exile for our entire life?

BALLABHA

If Maharaja wants to give in to this sinful and cowardly desire to hand over the earth to evil-minded Duryodhana, then why kill Kichaka in secret? I will kill him in broad daylight, and then we can all reveal ourselves and go back into further exile.

KANKABHATTA

Bhima, it is not my wish to allow some ill-considered and aggressive action on our part to rout and humiliate us and thus force us back into forest exile. I want to get back the throne of Indraprastha so that I may have an opportunity to share with everyone in the world the understanding of dharma that emerged in us Pandavas during our exile. This true and fundamental duty of the Pandavas can only be fulfilled by one vow …

BALLABHA

Which vow is that?

KANKABHATTA

To not fall prey to greed or anger and thus get provoked into straying from dharma.

BALLABHA

After witnessing all that happened in the durbar this evening, Maharaja, why do you still think it is wrong to slay Kichaka? How can you still think, Maharaja, that Sudeshana's appeals, Ratnaprabha's pleadings, or the fear of Virata Maharaja will change Kichaka? Does Kichaka fear Virata? Or is it Virata who fears Kichaka? Dada, do you still have any doubts about the answer?

KANKABHATTA

Looking at Kichaka alone, I don't think it would be against dharma to slay Kichaka; but ...

BALLABHA

Again, but? But ... but ... but ...

KANKABHATTA

But, Bhima, the point is we have spent so many months under Raja Virata's protection. Won't killing Kichaka cripple the power of his Matsyadesha, and won't it sadden Raja Virata?

BALLABHA

Dada, won't our strength that kills Kichaka not also prove useful to Virata Raja? Dada, I know that after I slay Kichaka tonight, the Trigartas will no longer fear Matsyadesha. Then the Trigartas and the Kauravas will unite and campaign as one against Matsyadesha. But, Dada, that's when we Pandavas will send the Trigartas and the Kauravas packing! Once that happens, won't Raja Virata forget Kichaka's slaying and start loving us complete.

KANKABHATTA

That will surely happen; but, Bhima, it would be much better if the Pandavas can win Raja Virata's affection without slaying Kichaka. Bhima, Kichaka is an able and proud man, and there is only one remedy to soften such men. If you show them strength greater than theirs – or some strength rooted in dharma – they return to the path of virtue on their own. Bhima, show your tremendous strength to Kichaka and entreat him to come to the side of the Pandavas.

BALLABHA

I will do all of that. Dada, now let me go. This conversation will delay my getting to the Bhairava temple.

KANKABHATTA

Go, go quickly. May all the gods give you their strength. But, Bhima, don't use this strength to kill Kichaka if he comes back to his senses.

BALLABHA

No, Dada, my hands will never commit such a sin.

(Leaves)

KANKABHATTA

Oh god, when Bhima seizes Kichaka to kill him, don't let any false sense of honor govern Kichaka's mind, and let him come over to the Pandavas' side and make the Pandavas' exile in Virata Nagari peaceful for the Pandavas and prosperous for Virata Raja.

(Leaves)

Scene 2

Place: Front courtyard of Kichaka's palace. Enter: Kichaka, Chanchala and Chapala.

KICHAKA

Chapala, take my bow and arrows inside; also take this quiver.

CHAPALA

Then, Maharaja, shall I bring the mace?

KICHAKA

No, I don't need the mace. Go, I don't need this Mahashankha either. Put it inside as well.

CHAPALA

Maharaja, if you are not taking any weapons, shall I at least bring the armor?

KICHAKA

No, nothing; now leave. *(Chapala leaves with the bow and arrows)* Chanchala, keep this sword. I don't even want this with me. Go and see if the chariot has been brought; find out what's going on. I have been standing in this courtyard for such a long time. Keep the sword inside, and enquire about the chariot. *(Chanchala begins to go)* Chanchala, come here; first find out from the guard whether or not we have received word of Sairandhri's arrival at the forest temple.

CHANCHALA

What's this Maharaja! The guard confirmed that Sairandhri had been escorted to the forest, and only then did Maharaja order the charioteer to keep the chariot ready.

KICHAKA

Oh, I forgot! I was so lost in thought about how I will embrace Sairandhri in the Bhairava temple in the forest that I couldn't remember. Go put the sword away and find out about the chariot. *(Chanchala starts to go)* Chanchala, come back for a minute. Look for two garlands on the bed made for me and your mistress, and bring them here.

CHANCHALA

Yes, Maharaja. *(She begins to go but turns back)* But Maharaja, if Maharani Saheb comes in right then and asks me not to touch the garlands, what shall I do?

KICHAKA

Chanchala, you're such a worrying type! If this happens, or that happens, what shall I do? Sit and cry! Imagine the worst fears, and sit and worry. Just go and get the garlands. *(Chanchala goes)* For my meeting with Sairandhri I was needlessly and foolishly carrying my weapons with me. With a proud woman like Sairandhri and a powerful man like me, once I put my hand on hers in private, we will be united as if we are tied together with a garland of flowers. *(Chanchala come back)* You've returned halfway through the task! That's most inauspicious! No matter what she's told to do, it's impossible that this crybaby will do it without some sulk or the other! Now crybaby, what will you cry about? Answer; answer!

CHANCHALA

Maharaja, the fear I had felt in my heart was not entirely unwarranted. Look there, Ratnaprabha Rani Saheb is coming here. So how can I bring the garlands?

KICHAKA

Once a crybaby, always a crybaby. You have no initiative. Chanchala, if she comes here, it will be easier for you to go there. Go to the bed and take the garlands directly to the chariot. Go and don't scrunch up your face …

CHANCHALA

But now will Maharani Saheb allow Maharaja to go out?

KICHAKA

Who told you to mind my business? Go … go quickly. So inauspicious!

(Chanchala leaves, and Ratnaprabha enters)

Maharani Saheb, at this odd hour of the night what makes you take the trouble of stepping out of the palace on your tender feet? Please forgive the one guilty of making this enquiry, and may your Highness do him the favor of your command. Your servant is eager to serve you.

RATNAPRABHA

Maharaja, no matter how much you ill-treat and distance this poor dasi of yours, and no matter where and how you kick her, because of her selfless love for you she will, no matter the odd hour of night or day, fall at these feet of yours and entreat you again and again.

KICHAKA

(Kneels) My beautiful dearest, before you pronounce your command, please allow me a little time. *(Rises)* Soon I will bring Sairandhri here to supplicate at your feet.

RATNAPRABHA

It will pain your heart, so how can I tell you that the act you are going to commit is a sin? To criticize Maharaja is not proper for me. But Maharaja *(falls into Kichaka's arms)* your family is renowned in this Matsyadesha for ancestors who were righteous, feared sin, and followed dharma. That this dasi has reminded you now of your virtuous ancestors' glory will, I hope, not displease you? Even your own character until today has been so very pure! Maharaja, resist your headstrong insistence on fulfilling your sinful pledge and avoid disgracing the Kichaka-Anu-Kichaka clan and destroying yourself and your family.

Kichaka-Vadha (The Slaying of Kichaka, 1907)

KICHAKA

(Frees himself from her and moves away)

Ratnaprabha, it is my misfortune that you are incapable of understanding the deep affront – the sense of injury to my reputation – that is racking my mind. It's not enough for women to be beautiful, loving and discreet. If they don't have the intelligence to understand their husband's sense of honor and dishonor, then the world of brave and great men who live with such women remains a sad and unhappy one. This conviction of learned men, Ratnaprabha, with your behavior now you have shown to be quite right.

RATNAPRABHA

Maharaja, I lack intelligence; that's true; but I have become righteous in your company, and so I fall at your feet and implore you. He who made Mount Kailasha shudder and who with his own might imprisoned three hundred and thirty million gods and made them all perform household chores in his palace, even that twenty-armed Raja Ravana's false notions about his own power – about his honor and dishonor – his acclaim and insult – led to his destruction. He kidnapped Sita mistaking her to be an ordinary woman. Not that he found Sita any more beautiful than Mandodari, nor did he love saintly Mandodari any less than he loved Sita. But he thought he would lose his reputation if he released Sita, and so he remained obstinate and kept battling Rama and lost everything. Maharaja, I don't have much knowledge, and I don't have the intellect to know how best to implore you at your feet. Still because of my pure love for you, I will take the risk of making this request. I was just reading in my palace Mandodari's last appeal to Ravana to release Sita as he was leaving for war in the Story of Rama. Wait here for just a moment. I will bring the book and read Mandodari's entreaty for Maharaja. Whosoever hears that appeal, his mind cannot remain unchanged, I am confident of that.

KICHAKA

Go; whatever books you have, bring them all. I will go through those books and assure you that although this Kichaka is more capable than Ravana, Sairandhri is not fit even to be the dust under Sita's feet. Go; bring all the books; don't leave a single book behind, so that I'll be free of the constant niggling of these books once and for all!

(Ratnaprabha goes)

Foolish Ratnaprabha, the man who was notorious for saying one thing one moment and its opposite the next, the man who went back on his word so constantly that people dubbed him "Ten-Headed," if that Ravana did not change his decision because of Mandodari's sermon, how can you think that the same sermon will cause this man-of-his-word, this steadfast Kichaka, to go back on his pledge? Foolish, truly foolish! The gods in the sky look down on the earth and always shed tears as they discuss among themselves the faults of human beings. Now all the twinkling stars in the sky – the eyes of the gods – will be shedding special tears, not from sorrow but from laughter at your foolishness.

(Chanchala enters)

CHANCHALA

Your Highness, the garlands have been placed in the chariot, and the charioteer is all set.

KICHAKA

Chanchala, earlier your arrival brought a bad omen for me, but this time your arrival has brought a bad omen for Ratnaprabha; so here's a reward for you. *(Gives her a necklace)* Your mistress is coming here from the palace, but before she gets here I am leaving. Tell her that instead of finding examples in books, I have gone to do the deed – to the forest to violate Sairandhri. Come, take me to the chariot.

CHANCHALA

Here … here … this way, Maharaja.

(They leave)

Scene 3

Place: Bhairava Temple in the Devi Forest. Sairandhri lies unconscious.

SAIRANDHRI

(Regaining consciousness)

Looks like all the monsters have gone; left me here all alone! How long have I been unconscious? Is anyone other than Bhairava here in the temple? Draupadi, look at your state! That evil Duhshasana tried to ruin me in the packed durbar; but Dhritarashtra miraculously came back to his senses and sent us off to exile. At least then this wife of the Pandavas was not alone. It's true that today Virata Maharaja stopped Kichaka from pulling off my pallava in the durbar, but then he arranged to have me sent all alone to the forest, so that I may be sacrificed to Kichaka! I was certain that Bhima Maharaja – the Slayer of Jarasandha, Bakasura, Kirmira, and other demons – will come to the forest to protect me, and so I did not scream in fear when Virata's guards brought me here. Now in the forest … whose footsteps are making those sounds? Hope it's not the devil Kichaka!

(Gets up; tries to listen)

Sounds like the footsteps of a brave man … my dear husband … the greatest in the world … the epitome of courage … the Bhairava of the battlefield … my dear …

(Kichaka enters with the two garlands around his neck)

KICHAKA

(Offers her one of his garlands)

To offer you this garland of love …

SAIRANDHRI

(Throws the garland away)

Demon, wherever you were hiding for so long, go back and stay there. What? You cannot hear the sound of approaching footsteps? To destroy wicked sinners like you, my beloved will …

KICHAKA

Now apart from this brave man, who is your beloved? Your talk of yakshas and kinnaras frightened Sudeshana and Ratnaprabha; your trick worked in front of women. But with this Bhairava as my witness … why bother with him as my witness … I regard this Bhairava as the servant who washes my bed linens and cleans my pot of spit …

SAIRANDHRI

Devil, insulting the gods like this?

KICHAKA

Nobody in this world can equal me. I am the foremost, and then there are all the other gods. Sairandhri, I am the god of gods. I am the king of kings. Consider me the lover of all the beautiful women of the world and allow me to take this garland from my neck and place it around your neck.

(He removes the second garland from his neck and begins to put it around her neck)

SAIRANDHRI

(Throws the garland away)

Get out, demon, your time is up. Don't throw yourself into the mouth of death deliberately.

KICHAKA

(Grabs her arm)

Enough of your stubbornness. Whether you like it or not, I am going to put you in my chariot just now and take you to my palace.

(Begins to drag her)

SAIRANDHRI

Beloved husband, help! Help! This wicked Kichaka is ruining Draupadi's honor ...

(Tries to free herself)

KICHAKA

What? Are you Draupadi? That's excellent. What Suyodhana could not achieve, I will realize today. Draupadi, ultimately you would have become my mistress after the great battle between the Kauravas and the Pandavas, but now you will be mine this very second. I kept thinking to myself that you must belong to a noble family, because how else would a great archer like me be attracted to a lowly maid?

SAIRANDHRI

Why hasn't he come yet! Beloved Bhima Maharaja, help! Help!

KICHAKA

Draupadi, now I understand who your saviors are, and now I remember that your hair was never braided. Don't even dream that Bhima will braid your hair with hands wet with the blood of Duhshasana. Before we embrace, let me braid your hair with my hands.

SAIRANDHRI

Beloved Bhima Maharaja, help! Help!

KICHAKA

Draupadi, you are going to become my mistress – god Brahma has etched this in clear letters in your and my destiny. This time become my lover willingly, and watch my mighty feats. I will enter the city and single-handedly battle the Pandavas who are living secretly in Matsyadesha. To make up for my mistake of not attending your swayamvara, I will bring the heads of all five Pandavas tomorrow and offer them at your feet, the feet of my lover.

SAIRANDHRI

Evil demon, until your head is offered at the feet of this Bhairava, this Draupadi will not leave this temple – understand it well. *(Goes close to Bhairava)* Bhairava Maharaja, kill this sinner and save this innocent creature from disaster.

KICHAKA

Draupadi, to free you from my custody, what power does this Bhairava have? Darling, if you want to see the miracle of power, command me. With my left hand I will grab his hair, and with a single blow to his chest with my right hand, I will crush his body and offer the helpless head of this Bhairava at your feet.

SAIRANDHRI

Wicked … savage … sinner … demon …

KICHAKA

Draupadi, how dare you abuse me? Control your tongue, or else …

SAIRANDHRI

(Stands on one side of Bhairava)

Demon, what do you think? Even if no one comes to help me in this place, I'm capable of teaching you a lesson myself.

KICHAKA

(Stands on the other side of Bhairava; with rage)

Draupadi, accept my wish willingly …

SAIRANDHRI

Bhima Maharaja, help! Help! Beloved Bhima Maharaja …

KICHAKA

Shout! Shout for Arjuna! Shout for Bhima! Let Arjuna come! Let Bhima come! The time has come for you to lose your pride in your pativrata and the Pandavas' pride in their might.

SAIRANDHRI

Help! Help! Beloved Bhima Maharaja, help!

KICHAKA

Draupadi, even if Arjuna – who gained his expertise in weapons from Shankara through great penance in the Himalayas – arrives here this second, I will take his life with just one kick and use his bows and arrows as a pillow for the bed on which you and I will make love. Even if your beloved Bhima – the one with the might of a thousand snakes – appears here right now, I will with these hands soaked in that arrogant man's blood untie the knot of your blouse. Draupadi, just so you realize how great my strength is, I will turn this stone into dust with just one blow.

(Moves his fist towards Bhairava's chest. Bhairava grabs Kichaka's wrist with one hand and his neck with the other hand and drags him towards the front)

BALLABHA

Kichaka, coward, if you have the guts, look at this Bhima. I am the one who's called Ballabha, and I am the one who's called Bhima. I am ready to sit on your throat and break all the bones in your neck. Demon, whatever final resolutions you have, make them now, but if even a word escapes your mouth, I will send you to the house of death.

KICHAKA

(Releasing himself)

Whether you are Bhairava or Bhima, I am ready to fight you in man-to-man battle. If you are Bhima, I will overpower you in combat. With one kick to your chest I will make your blood spurt from your heart, and with these mighty hands soaked in that blood I will violently braid Draupadi's hair. And I will expel your soul through your eyes, so that your last sight is of this Kichaka stopping you from fulfilling your pledge to braid Draupadi's hair with hands soaked in Duhshasana's blood. Come on, get ready to fight.

BALLABHA

(Seizes Kichaka's arm, throws him to the floor and sits on him)

You ass, are you my equal that I should battle with you? With one blow to your chest I will send you to the vultures. Dharmaraja has given me the order where, out of consideration for Ratnaprabha and Virata, if you meet certain conditions, your life may be spared. During our exile when Jayadratha tried to rape Draupadi, Dharmaraja spared his life only when he agreed to shave his head in three sections, go in a procession through the streets sitting on a donkey, and announce to everyone that he was Draupadi's slave. In the same way, if you are ready to declare in Virata's durbar that Sairandhri's protectors, the yakshas and kinnaras, have made you their slave, shaved your head in three sections, and thus spared your life – and if you agree to take a vow of silence about our disguise until our exile is over – then, Kichaka, for the sake of Ratnaprabha and Virata, according to Dharmaraja's orders, I will let you live.

SAIRANDHRI

Kichaka, don't look so sore that you will escape with your life solely because of your wife's virtues. For Ratnaprabha's sake I do not object to your life being spared.

KICHAKA

Become Draupadi's slave in order to remain alive! I would rather fight and remain alive, and carry Draupadi to my palace.

BALLABHA

Your palace now is where vultures swoop low.

KICHAKA

If you are a real Kshatriya, then let's battle with maces …

BALLABHA

Battle of maces now? Why a battle of maces? For a mosquito that can be crushed with a snap of my fingers, who brings a mace! Draupadi, since the Pandavas have no alternative but to slay Kichaka, I am dispatching him to the house of death.

(Strikes a blow to Kichaka's chest. Kichaka falls dead)

Draupadi, let's leave this forest and go to Dharmaraja in the city and then decide what to do next.

SAIRANDHRI

But, beloved, first tell me when did you come here?

BALLABHA

I came to the forest as soon as I got Dharmaraja's final orders about slaying Kichaka. If by chance someone noticed me in the forest, I wanted them to think that some divine power had killed Kichaka, so I disguised myself as god Bhairava. And just then I saw Kichaka in his chariot, without his crown, looking intense, and hurriedly entering the forest. So I dashed here before him, and while you were unconscious, I picked up Bhairava's statue and hid it inside.

(Brings Bhairava's statue from within)

In its place I stood here, watched the unfolding events, and, as Dharmaraja had instructed, confirmed whether or not Kichaka would prove worthy of our offer to spare his life.

(Reinstalls Bhairava's statue)

Draupadi, bow to this Bhairava.

(Both bow)

Apply this holy ash to your forehead.

(Both apply ash to their foreheads)

Let's go, Draupadi, and tell Dharmaraja about all these events.

(They leave)

Curtain

KEY TERMS

aachari	Principal chef
aarti	Ritual circling of lamps before an idol or a person
adhiraja	Overlord among kings or princes
akka	Respectful term for one's elder sister or for an older female
Annam Brahmeti Vyajanat	Sanskrit expression equating food with Brahman or God
Anu-Kichakas	Kichaka's kinsmen and fellow caste members who constitute a powerful faction in Matsyadesha; also called *Upa-Kichakas*
bai	Respectful term for a lady, mistress, one's mother, or an elderly female
bhatt	Priest
Brihannada	Arjuna, one of the five Pandava brothers, disguised as a eunuch and serving as the music and dance teacher for the ladies of the Virata household
dada	Respectful term for one's elder brother or for an older man
darshana	Vision or glimpse of a deity, usually through its idol
dasi	Maid, servant; also: courtesan, concubine, slave
Dharmaraja	Another name for Yudhisthira; literally, King of Dharma
drishti	Ritual gaze or look towards a religious object or display
durbar	Royal court
Duryodhana	Leader of the Kaurava faction and the de facto king of Hastinapur; anoints himself Emperor of India. Also called Suyodhana and Kauraveshvara. In the interest of clarity for a broad audience, I use Duryodhana throughout, except in one section in Act 4 where Virata's play on the names requires "Suyodhana"
gulal	Red powder used in festivals and rituals
Hastinapura	Capital of the Kaurava kingdom
Indraprastha	Capital of the Pandava kingdom
-ji	Respectful suffix; e.g., the priest or Bhatt is addressed as Bhattji
kalash	Metal pitcher used in Hindu rituals
kinnaras	Supernatural beings, often half-man and half-horse

kumkum	Red powder for ritual and cosmetic use
Matsyadesha	Nation of the Matsyas
Matsyapuri	City of the Matsyas
natakashala	Dancing hall, playhouse, harem
namaskara	Common greeting
ovalani	Ritual waving of a platter with lamps in front of a person's face
pallava	End of the sari that drapes over the shoulder
puja	Ritual offering of water, fruit and flowers to a deity, accompanied by recitation of mantras
pundit	Brahmin priest; scholar or learned person
raja	King
Rajasuya yajna	Extended royal consecration ritual to anoint an emperor
Ramarajya	Golden age of Rama's reign
rani	Queen
saheb (or *sahib*)	Respectful suffix, used for either gender; e.g., *Bai Saheb*
sarathiputra	Son of a charioteer
shembedi	Offensive term; literally, filthy with nasal mucous
swayamvara	Ancient ceremony where the daughter of a royal house chose her husband from among invited suitors, often based on the outcome of a contest
toran	Wreath
vahini	Sister-in-law
Yavanas	Population of Greeks from Asia Minor in Bactria, an ancient region northwest of India
yakshas	Supernatural creatures connected to vegetation and other elements in nature

INDEX